SNOWDONIA
FOLK TALES

ERIC MADDERN

ILLUSTRATED BY SUE MYNALL

The
History
Press

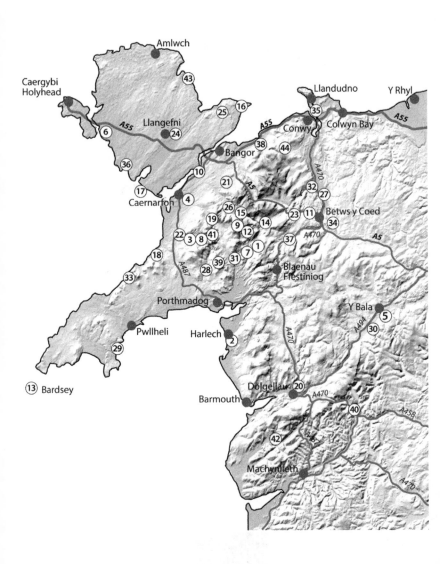

Amlwch

43

Caergybi
Holyhead

Llandudno

Y Rhyl

A55

35

16

25

A55

Conwy

Colwyn Bay

6

A55

Llangefni

38

44

24

Bangor

36

10

A470

17

21

A5

32

27

Caernarfon

4

26

15

23

11

Betws y Coed

19

14

34

22

3

8

41

9

12

A470

37

A5

18

31

7

1

A487

28

39

Blaenau
Ffestiniog

33

Porthmadog

Y Bala

5

A494

30

Pwllheli

Harlech

2

A470

29

13 Bardsey

Dolgellau

20

A470

Barmouth

40

A458

42

A487

Machynlleth

A470

LOCATIONS MAP

First published 2015

The History Press
The Mill, Brimscombe Port
Stroud, Gloucestershire, gl5 2qg
www.thehistorypress.co.uk

Reprinted 2016, 2017

British Library Cataloguing in Publication Data.
A catalogue record for this book is available from the British Library.

isbn 978 0 7524 9983 3

Typesetting and origination by The History Press
Printed in Great Britain by TJ International Ltd, Padstow, Cornwall

CONTENTS

Society *for*
Storytelling

Since 1993, the Society for Storytelling has championed the art of oral storytelling and the benefits it can provide – such as improving memory more than rote learning, promoting healing by stimulating the release of neuropeptides, or simply great entertainment! Storytellers, enthusiasts and academics support and are supported by this registered charity to ensure the art is nurtured and developed throughout the UK.

Many activities of the Society are available to all, such as locating storytellers on the Society website, taking part in our annual National Storytelling Week at the start of every February, purchasing our quarterly magazine *Storylines*, or attending our Annual Gathering – a chance to revel in engaging performances, inspiring workshops, and the company of like-minded people.

You can also become a member of the Society to support the work we do. In return, you receive free access to *Storylines*, discounted tickets to the Annual Gathering and other story-telling events, the opportunity to join our mentorship scheme for new storytellers, and more. Among our great deals for members is a 30% discount off titles in the *Folk Tales* series from The History Press website.

For more information, including how to join, please visit

www.sfs.org.uk

'Wales is noted for its tales of fancy ... A great place for spreading these tales was the special gathering known as *nosweithiau llawen* (pleasant evenings). A certain farmhouse would be fixed upon as the meeting-place, and the word would soon spread throughout the whole parish that ... a *noswaith llawen* would be held. The livelier section of the older men would take the lead, and the young men and women would gather round ... Drink and the harp were essential in these meetings; and once these enlivening elements had reached the heart and head of the orators, the evening would be considered in full swing. Lively songs were interspersed with amusing stories; the harpist would strike up one of the rousing Welsh melodies, and immediately a voice would chime in which spoke of love, of patriotism, or of deeds of bravery. He would then call for rest and a story. Then would one of the leaders call for silence, and the joviality would immediately cease. Every ear would attend to the *raconteur* while he related the story of the sport and daring of our forefathers and the feats of our ancestors on the battlefield. The magnificent pictures which were drawn of Arthur and his brave and noble knights roused the spirits of the young, and bred within them a courage and an independence which neither defeat nor tyranny could crush ...'

Bedd Gelert: Its Facts, Fairies and Folklore
by D.E. Jenkins (1899)

ACKNOWLEDGEMENTS

I'm grateful to the Ty Newydd Writers' Centre in Llanystumdwy for inviting Hugh Lupton and I to run retreats for storytellers over a twenty-year period. This gave us the chance to explore deeply many of the stories gathered in this book. I'd particularly like to thank Hugh, who has a deep knowledge of story and myth, and is a brilliant poet and storyteller. He always came up with an original idea that helped make these retreats extraordinary. One of our star guest speakers was Ronald Hutton. Thanks to him for his insight, inspiration and storytelling masterclasses. The tale of 'Gruffydd the Wanderer' is based on part of a talk he gave on the origins of *The Mabinogion*. Dafydd Davies-Hughes – master-craftsman, genius designer-builder, excellent storyteller – generously allowed us to tell stories in his Felin Uchaf roundhouse and has been a helpful mediator between me and the Welsh language and folklore. Gwyn Edwards has also kindly shared his local knowledge and passionate enthusiasm for the ancient mysteries of Wales. Thanks to Rob Collister, who has often guided me through these marvellous mountains; to Sue Mynall for her lovely illustrations; and to Alan Collinson, one of the last remaining professional cartographers in the UK, for his help with the map. I'd like to honour the memory of my Nain and Taid – Jane and Willie Evans from Pandy Tudur – without whom I'd never have landed in this wonderful part of the world; and also to thank my mum and dad, Alwena and Ralph Maddern, who passed on Taid's tales and whose enthusiasm for Snowdonia has never waned. And behind them, all the raconteurs and 'lively older men' who kept the tales alive until they could be written down in a bibliography of books. Thanks, too, to Angharad, whose love for Wales and for me has been a tremendous support. Finally, gratitude to Snowdonia itself, equal to any grand landscape in the world. I hope I have given it and its people a voice in this book.

Eric Maddern, 2015

ABOUT THE AUTHOR

eric maddern   was born in Australia but, after a ten-year journey around the world, made his home in the foothills of Snowdonia. There he and his friends created Cae Mabon, a unique and magical eco-retreat centre. He is also a storyteller and has told tales at historic sites around England and Wales and co-led courses for storytellers on the 'Matter of Britain'. He has written children's picture books and recorded two albums of his own songs.

INTRODUCTION

'Of all our native hills, Snowdon has the most astonishing wealth of
cultural texture, which in itself argues long attraction ... No other
mountain I know of – [then the names of eleven world-famous
peaks] ... nor any other of humanity's holy and legendary hills –
come with quite so much story attached.'

Snowdon: The Story of a Welsh Mountain by Jim Perrin (2012)

❧

Herein lie many of the stories 'attached' to Snowdon – and the
surrounding land of Eryri (Snowdonia), Ynys Môn (Anglesey) and
the Llŷn Peninsula. In short, the whole area covered by the old
Kingdom of Gwynedd – from the Great Orme to Bardsey Island,
from Bala Lake to Holyhead.

This landscape is staggeringly beautiful. Extraordinary places exist
here. It has been the canvas for human endeavour for thousands of
years. Despite peripheral intrusions of modernity much of the wilder
country has changed little in that time. In many areas it's possible to
see traces earlier peoples have left – standing stones, burial mounds,
hut circles, hill forts, house platforms, field boundaries, mottes and
castle keeps. Standing among the ruins of these ancient times can
be frustrating. I, for one, long to know more about the passions and
beliefs of the people who lived back then, about the spirit that moved
them to do what they did. And yet the stones are silent. Archaeologists

can be of some help, but they are reluctant to go 'beyond the evidence', to venture into the realm of the imagination. That's where the stories come in. The myths, legends and folk tales that have survived are windows into the worlds of our ancestors. A selection of such tales from Snowdonia is what you hold in your hand right now.

Most of the stories in this book have descended though the oral tradition. They are offered in roughly chronological order. The oldest, which came to be written down in *The Mabinogion*, reach back into prehistory and reveal glimpses of the mythic passions and practices of our Neolithic and Bronze Age forebears. There are also hints of the Druids – whose heartland was Ynys Môn – in, for example, the account of wizards who made a woman from flowers; the quest for the imprisoned 'great son of the great mother'; Gwion Bach's transformations through hare, salmon, bird and wheat on his way to becoming the inspired poet, Taliesin.

An excerpt from the oldest story mentioning Arthur is here, along with other tales the Welsh bards told to keep the Arthurian legend firmly planted in Snowdonia. Magic, mystery, weirdness, hilarity, beauty and sorrow abound. There is even a prophecy uttered by Merlin 1,500 years ago which seems to be coming true today. The saints were hot on the heels of Arthur – indeed one of them allegedly met him – and their lives give a flavour of the courage and determination of those early holy men and women. Despite Christianity's best efforts, a belief in fairies persisted even until now. Stories of encounters with the Tylwyth Teg have shown remarkable resilience.

Some Snowdonia folk tales are versions of stories found elsewhere, most famously 'The Faithful Hound', now associated with Beddgelert. Others are uniquely homegrown. A couple were passed down through the oral tradition to me from my Welsh grandfather, William Owen Evans. The final swathe of tales in the book are of legendary characters from history who have left a profound mark on this land and its people.

Although Ynys Môn was the Druid heartland, the mountains were their hinterland. To these peaks and passes they must have come for retreat and spiritual practice. Here they had their outliers, their border guards. So in the epilogue, inspired by the burial chamber Maen y

Bardd, the Poet's Stone, I've imagined a progression of characters who, over 5,000 years, have walked through 'the Pass of the Two Stones' on their way from the east to the Druid's Isle, just over the horizon …

There is no doubt that Eryri has always been a place of refuge – most famously when Vortigern fled from the Saxons to Dinas Emrys – but also a stronghold. With its dense forests, hidden valleys, caves and rocky crags, there are plenty of good places to hide … and to launch ambushes from.

Curiously, two of the more mythic tales suggest ancient links between Snowdonia – a place of raw physical power – and London, since time immemorial the centre of political power. The dragons, whose screams every May eve sent people mad and withered the land, were captured from the centre of the land by King Lludd and carried to Eryri where their disturbing power was contained in a lake below the summit of Snowdon. The giant king Bran, who came from Old Gwynedd, had his head buried under the White Mount (Tower of London) to protect the Island of the Mighty from invasion. These peripheral mountains can, it seems, both hold the troubles of the centre and send protection back to it!

Many years ago I worked in the Aboriginal communities of Central Australia. I came to understand a little of their complex and mysterious notion of 'the Dreaming'. To simplify, it works like this. In the beginning songlines and sacred sites were created by the journeys and adventures of the spirit ancestors. The people travelled along those songlines ('walkabout') and made ceremonies in the sacred sites (dancing, singing, retelling the stories) to keep the spirit of the Dreamtime alive. This strengthened the performers, who 'became who they were at the beginning of time', and left the place in good heart. By this means Aboriginal people maintained a spiritual connection with the land and communion with their ancestors. White Australians, they observed, 'got no Dreaming'.

This made me think, if there was a 'white man's Dreaming', what would it be? Since returning to Britain in 1982, and mostly living in North Wales, I've been exploring that question. I've worked for English Heritage and CADW telling stories at more than fifty historic sites (including Avebury, Tintagel and Conwy Castle) to bring these places alive. And for twenty years Hugh Lupton and I led a series of storytelling retreats at Ty Newydd Writers' Centre near Criccieth on 'the Matter of Britain'. Every year we spent at least a day visiting places in the landscape that related to the tales we were retelling. Four times, for example, we visited sites associated with the Fourth Branch of *The Mabinogion*, the story I've called 'The Wizards of Gwynedd'. We found that telling the story in the place it happened lights up both the tale and the place. The storyteller is invigorated and the place seems to come alive too. There is an echo here of the ceremonies Aboriginal people do to keep the spirit of the Dreaming alive.

This collection of tales arises, then, out of this prolonged period of exploration. It is my first stab at the 'White Man's Dreaming'! Of course the stories do not cover the whole of Britain. Far from it. But I believe they are representative of the larger material and, in my biased opinion, are as good as those to be found anywhere. I am, I freely admit, partisan in my view.

The longer I've lived in Wales and the more steeped I've become in these stories, the more Cymraeg I've felt. However, one of my regrets is that, despite some efforts, I've not mastered the Welsh language. This is a significant lack because Snowdonia is the heartland of the Welsh language and I know there are still traditional tales not yet translated into English. So I apologise to my Welsh friends and readers for that. I hope that what I have managed partly compensates.

I have, however, had my Welsh-speaking informants. Chief among them are Angharad Wynne, my partner, and Alwena Maddern, my mum. Angharad has generously shared her encyclopaedic knowledge of Wales and Mum has sent me handwritten translations of Welsh stories. Thanks very much to you both. My gratitude also goes to my father, Ralph Maddern, who, years ago, wrote half a dozen books about walking in Snowdonia. His love for the place shines through in these works. When I excitedly told him recently about my discoveries in the mountains he simply said, 'Yes, there is no better place in the world.'

Eric Maddern
Cae Mabon, Snowdonia, 2015

WELSH
PRONUNCIATION GUIDE

Pronouncing the 7 vowels

A –	'a'	as in man
E –	'eh'	as in bed
I –	'ee'	as in knee
O –	'o' (flat)	as in got
U –	'i'	as in bitter
W –	'oo'	as in zoo

Y can be said in three different ways:

'uh'	is used when it means 'the', e.g. 'y garn' (uh garn)
'ee'	when in the middle of words 'byd' (b-ee-d)
'u'	as in up, e.g. 'ynys' (un-ees)

Consonants to note

C –	'k'	as in kale
Ch –	'ch' (in throat)	as in the Scottish 'loch'
Dd –	'th'	as in breathe
Ff –	'f'	as in fellow
F –	'v'	as in very
G –	'g' (always hard)	as in good
NG –	'ng'	as in finger
R –	'rr' (rolled)	

Ll –   is a unique sound to Welsh and is formed by placing the
         tip of the tongue on the back of the top front teeth and
         forcing air between the tongue and the cheeks.

Pronouncing the dipthongs

Ae –	'y'	as in why
Ai –	'y'	as in why
Au –	'y'	as in why
Aw –	'ow'	as in how
Ei –	'ay'	as in day
Eu –	'ay'	as in day
Ew –	'eh-oo'	(no English equivilant)
I'w –	'ee-oo'	as in yew
Y'w –	'ee-oo'	as in yew
Oe –	'oy'	as in toy
Ow –	'oh'	as in low
Wy –	'oo-ee'	as in the French 'oui'
Ywy –	'ui'	as in Druid

Pronounciation of names

Arianrhod	a-rr-ee-ah-n-rr-h-od
Afagddu	a-v-a-g-th-ee
Beddgelert	b-eh-th-g-eh-l-eh-r-t
Bendigeidfran	b-eh-n-d-ee-g-ay-d-v-rr-a-n
Blodeuedd	bl-o-d-ay-eh-th
Blodeuwedd	bl-od-ay-oo-eh-th
Bwlch y Ddeufaen	b-oo-l-ch / uh / th-ay-v-iy-n
Ceridwen	k-eh-r-i-d-oo-eh-n
Creirwy	k-rr-ai-rr-oo-ee
Culhwch	k-i-l-hoo-ch
Cymru	k-uh-m-rr-ee
Dinas Emrys	d-ee-n-a-s / eh-m-rr-ee-s
Drws y Coed	d-rr-oo-s / uh / k-oy-d
Eryri	eh-rr-uh-rr-ee
Goewin	g-oy-oo-ee-n
Gronw Pebyr	g-rr-o-n-oo / p-eh-b-uh-rr

Gruffydd ap Cynan	g-rr-i-ff-i-th / a-p / k-uh-n-a-n
Gwenhwyfar	g-oo-eh-n-h-oo-ee-v-a-rr
Gwrhyr	g-oo-rr-hee-rr
Gwyddno	g-oo-i-th-n-o
Illtud	i-LL-t-i-d
Lleu Llaw Gyffes	LL-ee-oo / LL-ow / g-uh-ff-e-ss
Lludd	LL-ee-th
Llyfelys	LL-uh-v-eh-l-ee-s
Llywelyn	LL-uh-oo-e-l-uh-in
Llyn	LL-ee-uh-n
Llyn Cerrig Bach	LL-ee-n / k-eh-rr-igg / b-a-ch
Machynlleth	m-a-ch-uh-n-LL-eh-th
Maelgwn Gwynedd	m-iy-l-g-oo-n / g-oo-i-n-eh-th
Maen y Bardd	mah-en / uh / b-a-rr-th
Matholwch	m-a-th-o-l-oo-ch
Mawddwy	m-ow-th-oo-ee
Medrawd	m-eh-d-rr-ow-d
Mur Castell	m-i-r / k-a-s-t-eh-LL
Myrddin	m-uh-rr-th-i-n
Nantlle	n-a-n-t-LL-eh
Owain Glyndwr	o-oo-a-ee-n / g-l-i-n-d-oo-rr
Pryderi	p-rr-uh-d-eh-rr-ee
Rhitta	rr-hee-t-a
Taliesin	t-a-l-ee-eh-s-i-n
Tangwystl	t-a-n-g-oo-i-s-t-l
Twrch Trwyth	t-oo-rr-ch / t-rr-oo-ee-th
Tylwyth Teg	t-uh-l-oo-i-th / t-eh-g
Ynys Enlli	uh-n-i-s / eh-n-LL-ee
Ynys Môn	uh-n-i-s / m-or-n
Yr Wyddfa	uh-rr / oo-i-th-v-a
Ysbaddaden	uh-s-b-a-th-a-d-eh-n

1

MYTHIC ROOTS

The first stories in this book – with one exception – are some of Britain's oldest. By the time they were written down – in the twelfth and thirteenth centuries – they'd passed through the minds of many bards for more than 1,000 years. They were collected into a book we call *The Mabinogion* (sometimes *Mabinogi*), which has been described as 'mythology in decline'. Incomplete though it is, it's still possible to see traces of Bronze Age gods and goddesses, even to glimpse fragments of ancient creation myth. Through this we get hints of what the Celtic mysteries might have been. Bran, for example, is the sacred wounded king whose severed head brings about otherworldly enchantment but which eventually must be returned to the sacred land to ensure fertility and protection. Arianrhod, whose name means 'silver wheel', is a star goddess. Gwydion, wizard, trickster and storyteller, might be god of the bards. The stories of Math, son of Mathonwy, and his heir Lleu Llaw Gyffes, contain themes like betrayal, death and resurrection which were further developed in the Arthuriad. The Cauldron of Inspiration was later to become the chalice of the Holy Grail.

The one new story is 'The Druid Prince'. It is included here because it's set when the other stories were fully known and current. It draws on archaeological evidence and speculation about Lindow Man, the preserved body found in a peat bog near Manchester. Accepting the idea that it was a triple sacrifice I've constructed a narrative to highlight the significance of Ynys Môn in the clash between the Druids and the Romans in ad 60.

How the Dragons Were Buried at Dɪɴᴀs Emrys

Back in the swirling mists of time was a king, Beli Mawr, Beli the Great. He was king of the Britons before the Romans ever set foot on this land. His eldest son was Lludd, his youngest Llefelys.

When Beli died Lludd (known in the English tongue as Lud) became king of the Island of Britain. He was a wise and generous king and during his reign the people prospered. He rebuilt the broken walls of the greatest city, studding them with painted towers and making a grand gate, known as Lud's Gate or Ludgate. He encouraged the citizens to build splendid houses and dwelt there himself much of the year. Indeed the city was named after him: Caer Lludd. Later it became Lud's Town, then simply London.

After many years Lludd's luck changed. Three terrible plagues hit the land. The first was the curse of gossiping – no matter what secret was whispered into the ear of another it was caught by the wind and carried far and wide across the land. The second was the curse of gluttony – whenever ample provisions were gathered in the king's court, by the morning all had disappeared no matter how well guarded. But the third plague was the most terrifying of all. It was the curse of withering. On May eve every Beltane an awful scream was heard across the land, a scream that rose from the depths of the earth and sucked the sense and strength from every living thing. Old men who heard it went mad. Women lost their beauty and their babies died inside them. Children were struck dumb and healthy men withered on the spot. Animals and trees were left barren. The country became a wasteland.

This is how Lludd cured this worst curse. His younger brother Llyfelys had married the daughter of the King of France and by now was king himself. He was a wise man and Lludd knew he could help. So he put out to sea to meet his brother on the rolling waves of the channel between the two lands. Aboard a rocking boat Llyfelys insisted they talk through a long bronze horn so their secrets would not be whipped away by the winds. And so Llyfelys gave Lludd the remedies for all three plagues.

After dealing with the first two, Lludd followed his brother's instructions to remedy the third. The cause of this plague, Llyfelys had said, was two dragons – residing in the heart of the land – who every year battled to achieve supremacy. 'When the dragons are awake,' said Llyfelys, 'there is a disturbance in the land.' So Lludd had the Island of Britain measured in length and breadth and found its centre to be at Oxford. Then he loaded a wagon with a cauldron, two stone jars, a silken cloth the colour of mud and gallons of sweet, dark mead. On May eve he came to that central place. There he found a murky lake and a circle of standing stones. He wedged the cauldron in thick mud by the lake, filled it with the mead and covered it with the cloth. Next he went into the stone circle, pressed wax earplugs into his ears, and lay on the ground to wait. As the darkness coiled around him the air thickened and from under the earth came an awesome shudder. Lludd could hear nothing but he knew the scream had begun. Then from the lake he saw two monstrous water serpents rise up from the deeps, water dripping from their scales. The two serpents, one red, the other white, fought with each other, writhing and rolling in the mud. After the first round they sprouted horns and turned into shaggy oxen, charging at each other, screaming in pain. And so the battle continued through many shapes until at last they assumed their true form: snorting, fire-breathing dragons. Up into the air they rose, clawing at each other, snapping and snarling, until at last, exhausted from their efforts, they transformed into two piglets and fell back to earth, through the mud-coloured cloth and into the waiting cauldron. There they drank the mead and fell into the deepest sleep.

Lludd had no time to lose. He ran to the cauldron, snatched up the sleeping piglets and popped each one into a stone jar and placed them on his cart. Then he rode day and night to the strong-est, most secure place in his kingdom, Eryri, the mountains of Snowdonia. Finally he came to a hill called Dinas Ffaraon (later known as Dinas Emrys) just below Yr Wyddfa, the highest moun-tain in the land. There, in the hollow summit of the hill, he found a pool. With all his strength he lifted the two stone jars and hurled them into the rush-fringed pond. As they splashed into the water the small lake was itself swallowed up by the earth, leaving nothing but grass and stones rippling out in all directions.

And so the dragons were buried beneath the hill of what was to become Dinas Emrys. It would be hundreds of years before they would wake up again. Lludd's act became known as one of the 'Three Fortunate Concealments of the Island of Britain'.

Let He Who Would Lead be a Bridge

The Second Branch of The Mabinogion

Bendigeidfran – Bran the Blessed – was the giant high king of the Island of the Mighty. One day he was sitting with his court on the rock of Harlech looking out to sea when he saw thirteen ships approaching from Ireland. He sent armed men to meet them and discovered that Matholwch, the King of Ireland, had come seeking the hand of Bran's sister in marriage. She, Branwen, was the most beautiful girl in the world and became known as one of the 'Three Chief Maidens of this Island'. After taking counsel on the matter the union was agreed. Matholwch and his people sailed to Aberffraw on Ynys Môn while Bran and his retinue travelled overland. And there the wedding feast was held.

Bran had two half-brothers, the twins Nisien and Efnisien. Whereas Nisien would, where there was discord, bring harmony, Efnisien, where there was peace, would cause conflict. He was the bringer of bitter tears, which is perhaps why he was not invited to the wedding. However, when he discovered that his half-sister had slept with the King of Ireland, and that not only had he not been invited to the celebration, he'd not even been consulted about it, he was furious. He was determined to wreak revenge.

It was the horses that suffered most. They were fine, hand-picked steeds, specially brought over from Ireland for the occasion. They were an easy target. While the festivities were still in full swing, Efnisien crept through the shadows, a twisted but determined look on his face. A sudden flicker of silver in the moonlight and the horses were screaming in pain. He slashed tails to the back, ears to the skull, lips to the teeth. Even, where he could, eyelids were sliced off. Dodging flying hooves, oblivious to the whinnying terror, he slipped back into the darkness, grimly satisfied with his harvest of blood.

No matter what his big brother Bran might do to make amends with the offended Irish, there was only ever going to be an uneasy peace. Such a terrible action is not easily forgotten or forgiven. Only when Bran offered Matholwch the Cauldron of Rebirth (which could bring a dead man back to life, though without speech, and which had come originally from Ireland) did the Irish king disregard the insult of the maimed horses and rejoin the carousing. And the following day he sailed with his beautiful bride back to Ireland.

At first Branwen was warmly welcomed and gained much favour by giving valuable gifts to the nobles who visited the court. After a year she bore a son who was named Gwern. But thereafter she paid dearly for Efnisien's dark deeds. Her husband tried to love her, but the outraged voices of his countrymen grew from a whisper to a clamour. In the second year she was put from the royal bed and forced to work in the kitchen, where each day the butcher came to slap her on the face …

What's this? She has a bird in her hand. She is stroking its iridescent green and black feathers. Her hair is dishevelled, her face swollen, her beauty marred by bruising and distress. But she holds the bird, she loves the bird, she whispers to the bird: 'Go, my sweet starling, fly across the sea, go to my great crow-raven brother. His head is like a craggy mountain, his hair is a forest of spears, his eyes are bottomless pools. You will know him when you see him. His mind is full of the tales of our people. Go to him, to the ancient Druid, to mighty Bran. Tell him of his sister's fallen fortunes, call him to my aid.' And she throws the bird up into the air.

The starling flickers aloft, staggers upwards, beats its wings against the salt breeze, crosses the open water, seeks out its kin. It comes to the shining shore where the Eryri-fed waters of the Seiont river flow out to sea. And there, in the setting sun, it finds its flock. It penetrates the heart, sweeping and swirling, circling and diving, ten thousand birds ribboning together, the flock mind inscribing giant brush strokes across the sky, writing a message only an old Druid can read. Bran, looking up from his watching hill, sees the murmuration, reads the signs, recognises in the bird language a cry for help. He springs to his feet …

Bendigeidfran, Bran the Blessed, went with a mighty army to Ireland to rescue his sister and put wrongs to right. It was supposed to be a war to end wars. The giant king showed the way by laying

himself down over a river as a bridge so his people could cross, giving rise to the proverb 'let he who would lead be a bridge'.

But it did not end well. Efnisien's treachery led to further mayhem and the mayhem led to slaughter, wide and deep. Though the eagles may have flown high above Eryri foreshadowing victory for the Cymry, it was a hollow one. Bran was mortally wounded in the foot. Only Branwen and seven men – including Pryderi, Lord of Dyfed, the wise and cautious Manawydan, and Taliesin, Bard of the Shining Brow – made it back alive. Bran ordered that his head be cut off and carried, first around Wales, then to burial beneath the White Mount in London where it would, he said, protect the Island of the Mighty from invasion.

When they returned to their homeland Branwen was distraught. 'Woe that I was ever born,' she said. 'Two good islands have been laid to waste because of me.' And with that she let out a great sigh and her heart broke. She was buried in a four-sided grave on the banks of the Alaw river in Ynys Môn. The remains of Bedd Branwen, Branwen's Grave, can be found there to this day.

The journey around Wales was a time of enchantment. For seven years those who had returned from Ireland feasted in Harlech, accompanied by the Birds of Rhiannon. Though they could not see the birds the song rang in their ears as if they were close, utterly surpassing anything they'd heard before. So sweet was the music that all memory of sorrow and suffering was banished. What a blessed relief from grief it was. The enchantment continued on the Island of Gwales in the south where Bran's head was as good company as ever he had been. Never had life been more pleasurable. At this 'Assembly of the Noble Head', though time seemed to stand still, eighty years passed.

But one day one of the men decided to open 'the door to Cornwall' and as he did so all the memories of their losses and sufferings came flooding back. So they made their way to London and buried Bran's head on the White Mount. That act was another of 'the Three Fortunate Concealments of the Island of Britain'. From that day forth no invaders ever came across the sea to oppress the people of the Island of the Mighty. Not until, that is, Bran's Head was dug up. But that is another story.

The Wizards of Gwynedd

The Fourth Branch of The Mabinogion: The Wizard's Demise
From the summit of Snowdon west to the sea lies the Nantlle
Valley, the 'Valley of Lleu'. This story tells of the birth and strangely
charmed life of Lleu Llaw Gyffes – the Fair One with the Deft
Hand. But it is also about the wizard trickster Gwydion, his saga-
cious uncle Math, and Blodeuedd, the Woman of Flowers.

Math, son of Mathonwy ('Bear son of Bear-Like'), lived in Caer
Dathyl near the mouth of the Nantlle Valley. Many places have
been suggested as the location for this ancient hall. I think the
strongest contenders are Caer Engan, Y Foel and Craig y Dinas.
What is more certain is that Dinas Dinlle, an eroding hill fort
by the sea south of Caernarfon, was home to Math's nephew,
Gwydion, son of Dôn. Both men were wizards with consummate
powers.

Math had to live with a peculiar constraint. Unless he was at
war his feet had to rest in the lap of a virgin. Math's foot-holder
at the time was the beautiful Goewin, daughter of Pebin. While
Math was confined to his hall, his two nephews, Gwydion and
his brother Gilfaethwy, rode out with a retinue on a circuit of
Gwynedd making court visits.

It happened that Gilfaethwy developed a burning passion for
Goewin, but as she was never separated from Math he didn't
know what to do. She haunted his thoughts day and night until
he became sick with lust for her. Gwydion noticed this affliction
and asked his brother what was wrong. 'I cannot say,' replied
Gilfaethwy, 'for you know Math has the magical power to pick
up any word that is whispered on the wind.' 'Say no more,' said
Gwydion. 'I know what is troubling you. You love Goewen. Never
fear my lad, I will hatch a plan.'

Gwydion was not only a wizard, he was also a trickster and a
cunning fellow. But sometimes he was a fool who unleashed terrible
troubles. Now, merely for the sake of his brother's lust, he created war
among the Cymru which caused the death of many a hero. For war,
you'll remember, was the only way to separate Math from Goewin.

Gwydion went to Math and told him there were new beasts in the world called pigs. 'They are smaller than cattle,' he said, 'but their flesh tastes sweeter.' The only person in possession of these creatures, he explained, was Pryderi, Lord of Dyfed. He'd been given them as a gift by Arawn, King of Annwfn, the Otherworld. Math's appetite was whetted by this news so he asked Gwydion to obtain some of these animals.

Gwydion, Gilfaethwy and ten men went south to Pryderi's court in Ceredigion. They came in the guise of bards. As well as his other talents Gwydion was also a superb storyteller, the best in the world it was said. That night he wove a wonderful tale that enchanted all who heard it. 'You have a marvellous tongue,' was Pryderi's praise. Gwydion then admitted that his errand was to obtain the beasts from the Otherworld. 'Not easily done,' said Pryderi, 'for I have sworn neither to sell nor give them away until they have doubled their number.' 'Ah,' said Gwydion. 'In the morn I will show how you might exchange them with me.'

That night Gwydion resorted to his magical arts and conjured from toadstools twelve handsome steeds with bridles and saddles of gold, and twelve black and white-breasted hounds with collars and leashes of gold. The next morning Pryderi accepted these astonishing beasts in exchange for the pigs, and Gwydion and his companions set off with the sacred swine at once. 'We must make speed,' he said, 'for the spell will only last a day.' They headed north (leaving a trail of pig-named places such as Mochdre and Mochnant) eventually securing the animals in a sty high in the hills. When they returned to Caer Dathyl they found Math mustering his warriors for battle, for by then Pryderi had discovered Gwydion's trick and was heading north with his army, determined to seek vengeance.

Math and his men set out for the Glaslyn river estuary the next day, but that night Gwydion and Gilfaethwy secretly returned to Caer Dathyl. And in Math's very bed Gilfaethwy forcibly had his way with Goewin, and her maidservants were roughly thrown out of their quarters.

At dawn the two brothers rejoined their uncle's host and in the battles that followed a terrifying slaughter took place. The fighting

ranged up to Nant Coll near Beddgelert and back round to Dol
Benmaen. Finally Pryderi sent a message that the two sides should
desist and asked that the matter be settled between himself and
Gwydion, since he was the cause of the trouble. Gwydion agreed.
The two men met in single combat at the ford over the Glaslyn
river near where Maentwrog is today. By dint of his strength and
bravery, but also by using magic and enchantment, Gwydion was
victorious and Pryderi was slain. So ended the life of the renowned
leader of the southern cantrefs, all for the sake of Gilfaethwy's lust.
He was buried in Maentwrog and his smooth, rounded burial
stone still stands in the churchyard there, marking the last resting
place of Pryderi, one of the 'Three Powerful Swineherds of the
Island of Britain', the only character to appear in all Four Branches
of *The Mabinogion*.

On returning to Caer Dathyl, Goewin informed Math that
he would have to find a new foot-holder as she was no longer a
maiden. 'Your nephew Gilfaethwy raped me and shamed you,' she
said. 'Nor was I silent. There was no one in the house who did not
hear my cries.' Math took Goewin by the hand and said, 'I will do
right by you. I will make you my wedded wife and queen of my
kingdom.' But Gwydion and Gilfaethwy he outlawed, forbidding
his people to give them food and shelter. At last they came to his
court and set themselves at his will. 'If it were my will,' said Math,
'I would not have lost so many men in battle. Nor would I have
wished Pryderi's death, nor Goewin shamed as she has been.'

With that he took his magic wand and struck Gilfaethwy,
turning him into a hind, then Gwydion, turning him into a stag.
Making the punishment fit the crime he ordered them away to
mate in the manner of wild beasts. In a year's time barking dogs
announced the arrival of a pair of deer with a healthy fawn. Math
turned the fawn into a boy called Hyddwn. The hind he transformed into a wild boar, the stag into a wild sow, and sent them
off into the hills. A year later the dogs proclaimed the arrival of
the wild boar, sow and a good-sized piglet, which Math turned
into a boy called Hychddwn. Now Math transformed the sow
into a wolf, the boar into a she-wolf. At the end of the third

year they returned with a strong wolf cub, which became a boy called Bleiddwn. At last he turned his nephews back into their own shapes, believing that they had been punished enough and, he hoped, cured of their unbridled lust. He ordered them to bathe and to take fresh clothes. Then they were to come before him as friends again.

The Coming of the 'Fair One with the Deft Hand'

Math still hadn't found a new lap-maiden. With his nephews restored he asked their advice on where to find a suitable virgin. Gwydion suggested his own sister, Arianrhod, daughter of Dôn, the Silver Wheel of Fortune. When she was brought before Math he asked if she was a virgin. 'As far as I know,' she replied. To test her Math asked her to step over his magic wand. As she did a fine boy child with yellow hair fell from her loins. The boy uttered a loud cry and Arianrhod made for the door. As she did a second bundle dropped. Before anyone could get a look Gwydion snatched it up, wrapped it in a cloth and hid it in a chest at the foot of his bed.

Math named the yellow-haired boy Dylan. As soon as he heard his name the lad ran two miles to the sea and dived in, assuming the sea's nature and swimming as well as any fish. Later he became the Welsh Neptune and King of the Sea. The place where he plunged into the waves is marked by a large rock on the beach south of Dinas Dinlle, still known as Maen Dylan, Dylan's Rock.

Some time later Gwydion heard a cry from his magical chest. He opened it and saw an infant boy thrusting out his arms. He struck a bargain with a woman in the village to suckle the child and in a year's time he was like a two year old. At two years he was big enough to go by himself to court and at four people thought he seemed bigger than an eight year old. One day Gwydion took the boy to Caer Arianrhod. She asked after him and Gwydion said, 'He is a son of yours.' But Arianrhod was angry and ashamed. 'What is his name?' she asked. 'As yet he has none,' replied Gwydion. 'Then I will swear a destiny upon him,' spat out the goddess, 'that he shall never have one … unless I give it to him, which I never shall!'

Gwydion was undaunted by this curse. The next day he went with his 'son' to the seashore and, employing magical powers, conjured up a boat from dulse and sea-girdle. From the seaweed he made soft, beautiful, coloured leathers then sailed to the gate of Caer Arianrhod. There, taking on the semblance of a shoemaker, he began to fashion and stitch wonderful shoes. When Arianrhod saw them she sent her foot measurements so that shoes might be made for her. The first pair Gwydion deliberately made too large, the second pair too small. At last he said, 'I cannot make shoes for her unless I see her foot.' So she came to him at the boat. And Gwydion, one of the 'Three Golden Shoemakers of the Island of Britain', set about making her shoes. But at that moment a wren alighted on the prow of the boat. The boy picked up a stone and hurled it, striking the wren's leg between the tendon and the bone. 'My,' exclaimed Arianrhod, 'the fair one has a deft hand.' 'Aha!' said Gwydion. 'And now he has a name too. Lleu Llaw Gyffes, the Fair One with the Deft Hand, the Son of Light.' Arianrhod was furious at being tricked. As the boat and leather melted back into seaweed and dulse she swore a second curse: 'That he shall never bear arms and be a man … unless I equip him myself, which I never shall.'

Undeterred Gwydion again resorted to trickery to overcome the curse. He and Lleu went to Caer Arianrhod, this time in the guise of poet-storytellers. In the morning, after entertaining Arianrhod and her court the night before, he conjured up the semblance of a sea-borne fleet which, with the sound of trumpets and shouts, seemed intent on attacking the Caer. Arianrhod rushed to their chamber and begged the bard and his apprentice to help. 'We're short of men,' she said. 'Lady,' said Gwydion, 'I hear the clamour of men approaching. Quick. Let weapons be fetched. I will arm myself. You arm the youth.' 'Gladly,' she said. But as soon as Lleu had been armed the ships disappeared and the noise of attack faded away. Again Arianrhod had been tricked. She was furious. So for a third time she cursed her son. This time there was no 'unless I do it myself'. This time she swore that Lleu Llaw Gyffes would never have a wife from any living woman.

The Making and Unmaking of the Woman of Flowers

At first it seemed there would be no thwarting Arianrhod's third curse. But Gwydion knew Lleu would never be a fully initiated man unless he had a wife. So he brought Math into the plan and together they spiralled deep into their most powerful magic. They gathered the flowers of oak, broom and meadowsweet, never usually found together, and arranged them just so. For three days and nights they chanted powerful spells and incantations. On the last morning, beneath the heap of flowers, lit by rays from the rising sun, there she was … the naked body of a young woman, her eyes opening for the first time. Lleu was overjoyed with his bride and that night, after the wedding feast, they slept together. Because she was made of flowers she was called Blodeuedd, the Woman of Flowers.

It could have been so simple. Lleu, the son of the Sun, married Blodeuedd, daughter of the Earth. He with eyes shining like the sun on pools of water, his back straight as a sunbeam; she as beautiful as the flowers of the Earth, singing songs to the sky. But life rarely is that simple. In time a cloud crossed their skies and their lives twisted into tragedy.

Math gave Lleu the cantref of Ardudwy (stretching from Maentwrog toward Dolgellau) to be his lands. There he and Blodeuedd set up court in Mur Castell (known now as Tomen y Mur) and all seemed well. But Blodeuedd wasn't like other women. She'd heard about the laws of the land but she'd not grown into them. And though Lleu was kind to her and she liked him well enough, he never excited her. What she loved most was to go into the wildwood, to dance and sing. For at heart she was a tree spirit, a flower maiden. She left running court affairs to her senior women. Like a wild child she was more interested in mischief and play.

One day, when Lleu was away visiting Math and Gwydion, she heard the sounds of barking dogs, whinnying horses and shouting men as a hunt rode by her hall. The energy of the hunt excited her. Something about the raw, wild animality of it all set her pulse racing. After the hunters had felled the stag and baited the dogs she sent a messenger to invite them to dine with her. 'After all,' she said to her maidservants, 'it would be bad manners not to.'

The leader of the hunt – Gronw Pebyr, Gronw the Radiant – was Lord of Penllyn, a cantref which stretched from the mighty mountain Cadair Idris in the south, to the head of Llyn Tegid in the east and right up to the sharp-peaked Cnicht in the north. To the west Gronw's land adjoined Ardudwy, Lleu's province. Perhaps Gronw had not noticed when he crossed the border; perhaps there was something fated in the way the stag led them to Mur Castell.

Inside the hall Gronw took off his boots and riding jacket, loosened his shirt ties and sat by the rough-hewn table with a leather mug of mead. Blodeuedd admired his powerful build, his thick beard, his laughing brown eyes. As the fire crackled and the candles flickered all the others disappeared in a buzz of merry chatter. Gronw's eyes widened at the wonder before him. The woman of flowers. He'd heard of her beauty but in the flesh she was utterly entrancing. Her eyes, green as acorns, bewitched him. Her broom-yellow hair, loose over her shoulders, longed to be stroked. Her skin, creamy as meadowsweet, ached to be kissed. He was on fire. With no thought of consequences he reached out, drawn towards her delicate nectar like an intoxicated bee. Suddenly he was on his knees like a priest before his goddess. And she … said yes. She chose him, this half-wild man of beast and forest, and invited him into her bed.

They gave in to their passions all night long. He taught her so much of lovemaking. She showed him so much exquisite beauty. The next day, in a daze, he said he should leave but she said no, stay. His men long gone he stayed for a second divine night. But on the third day at last they talked of consequences. How can we live without this passion? We must be together. But what of Lleu? Come away with me. But he will seek us out. So he must be killed. That cannot be easily done. He is under a powerful protection. Find out the secret of his death. I will do it. Whatever it takes. For you …

Soon after Lleu returned to Mur Castell. But that night Blodeuedd was quiet and withdrawn. 'What's the matter, beloved?' asked Lleu.

'I've been worrying about you,' said Blodeuedd softly, 'and what would happen if you died.'

Lleu laughed. 'Don't worry about that. Unless God takes me I cannot be easily killed.'

'That's a relief,' said Blodeuedd. 'But, there is a way, is there? Perhaps you should tell me so I can be sure it doesn't happen. After all, a wife should guard her husband's safety.'

Lleu smiled, touched by his wife's care. 'Well it's all extremely unlikely,' he said. 'I can be killed neither inside nor outside, neither on foot nor on horseback.'

'I see what you mean,' said Blodeuedd. 'Sounds impossible.'

'Not only that,' added Lleu, starting to enjoy the impossibility of it all, 'I could only be killed by a spear that has been one year in the making, and then only on holy days.'

'So … is there a way someone could overcome all this?' asked Blodeuedd, reaching out and stroking Lleu's arm.

Lleu paused, looked at his sweetheart, took a deep breath and confided to her his deepest secret. 'If there was a thatched bathtub by the river, and if I was to stand with one foot on the side of the tub and the other on the back of a billy-goat, and if someone were to strike me with that year-in-the-making spear, then and only then would I die.'

'Good,' said Blodeuedd. 'That's not going to happen is it!'

But the next day she sent a message to Gronw to start work on the spear. For his part he felt as if he had drunk a witch's brew. He had only one choice. He'd never spent a year making a spear before. It would be the spear of spears. Taken from an ancient, bleeding yew, from a branch that was straight and true, Gronw whittled it down to the heart, hardened it in the fire, fletched it and tipped it with poison. After a year he sent the message: 'I'm ready.' Blodeuedd, for her part, had arranged for a thatched bathhouse to be built and had alerted the nearby goatherd.

Lleu was riding home from Caer Dathyl along the northern bank of the Glaslyn river. His horse knew the path and the reins lay slack in his hands. He came to a ford and the horse plunged in, the swirling river up to his boot heels. On the other bank Lleu glimpsed a smooth, rounded standing stone he knew well. Pryderi's tombstone. He'd heard the story of Gwydion's single combat with the Lord of the South, though not from Gwydion himself.

Occasionally he caught twisted mutterings about Gwydion, oaths carelessly uttered by those who'd lost loved ones in the battle. 'All for that stupid brother of his,' he once heard. 'Poor Goewin,' some of the women had said. Gwydion might be a clever wizard and a good storyteller but he was not liked by everybody. He'd been a good uncle to Lleu, though, helpful and loving. He'd taught him secrets he'd revealed to no other man. Maybe Gwydion was making up for his dark past in his love for Lleu.

Blodeuedd greeted Lleu with a smile and a gentle kiss. Soon he was busy giving orders to his men and later telling Blodeuedd the news from Math's court. He didn't notice anything different about her. That wasn't unusual. But inside Blodeuedd was different. For the first time in her fragile existence she was about to act. She was going to do something mighty. A chill breeze made the soft petals round her heart flutter and tremble. All the pieces of her plan were in place. Gronw had been told. Tomorrow was the day.

In the morning she squeezed Lleu's hand and said, 'It's midsummer's day. Let's go down to the river. I have a treat for you! Let me bathe you in my new bathhouse.' It sounded good. Lleu was tempted. Besides, he liked to humour his wife. As they walked down the earthen path birds sang, the summer flowers bloomed. A thatched roof perched over a new wooden tub full of steaming water. Her maidens had done as she'd asked. 'Come,' she said, helping him to slip off his clothes. With a deep sigh he sank into the fragrant water. She soaped his muscled back and shoulders, washed his hair. Lleu dissolved in the pleasure of it, never for a moment suspecting a thing.

Blodeuedd didn't fully comprehend what she was doing. She only knew that a strange memory of overwhelming desire was driving her on. She turned and nodded to the old goatherd who tethered a shaggy, long-horned billy by the side of the bathhouse. When Lleu was finished he stepped dripping out of the water and wrapped a cloth around his waist. 'Look, a goat!' she said. 'What did you say about standing on a bath and a goat? How funny! You could do it now. If it happened once it would never happen again. But how? You'd slip wouldn't you?'

'No,' said Lleu, entranced by the water, sun, flowers, her laughing voice, not hearing the bees buzzing around her heart … 'Like this.'

He rose up, one foot on the edge of the tub, the other, unsteady at first, on the back of the goat. She reached out her hand to steady him. Slowly he straightened to his full height. He took a deep breath. Through the oaks a shaft of sunlight fell upon him. Fresh, clean and invigorated he stood tall, let go of her hand and spread his arms. 'There, you see!'

A wren hopping in a hawthorn was chirping fiercely. A shadow fell across the sunbeam. Too late he saw the spear speeding towards him, sneering, heart-hungry and shaggy with barbs. Too late, too late. It pierced skin, flesh, bone, heart … He crumpled and for a moment was suspended in the air. Then a dark shape fell upon him with wings spread wide. Claws sank into his shoulders, his body was ebbing away, shrinking, failing, falling apart. The great bird flapped its wings once, twice, three times – as if lifting the Earth – then flew off through the trees and was gone.

She stood. Where was he? Was this what Death means? Not even a warm hand gone cold. Just emptiness, a space. What was this in the corner of her eye? She wiped away a tear and looked up. A dark, raging passion was running towards her. Ah yes, this was why. This was what it was for. He swept her up in his arms.

Gronw the Radiant and Blodeuedd, Woman of Flowers, went to Lleu's Hall and that night they slept together. The next day Gronw took possession of Lleu's land so that Ardudwy and Penllyn were under his control. For many weeks Gronw and Blodeuedd enjoyed being together. But as the weeks stretched into months a gnawing feeling grew in Gronw. He knew this couldn't last. He had murdered a man, a lord no less, and one beloved by two powerful men. Sooner or later they would be on his trail to exact revenge.

When Gwydion heard what had happened he set out to find his nephew. He wandered wide until he came to a house in Arfon where he heard from a swineherd about a sow that left her pen every morning and ran swiftly off. 'No one can catch her,' he said. 'No one knows where she goes.'

'Wait for me in the morning,' said Gwydion. At daybreak he was there and followed the sow briskly up the Nantlle Valley. She stopped under an oak tree and began to eat. When Gwydion got closer he realised to his dismay that she was devouring rotting flesh and maggots. He looked up into the tree and in the topmost branches spied an eagle. It did not look well. When it ruffled its feathers rotting flesh and maggots fell to the ground, so sustaining the sow. He sensed this bird was none other than Lleu, transformed and barely alive. So he sang an englyn, a powerful magical spell, and the eagle dropped half-way down the tree. He sang a second and it came into the lower branches. Finally a third englyn brought the bird before his feet. And there, with his magic wand, he turned it back into Lleu. But Lleu on death's door. He knelt down, scooped him up and carried him home. It took Gwydion a whole year, using all his healing powers, to bring Lleu back to health again. And when he did they knew the first thing they must do was to punish Gronw and Blodeuedd. Lleu wanted to take on Gronw. Gwydion said he'd deal with the Flower Maiden.

When Blodeuedd and her maidens saw Gwydion approaching Mur Castell they took off for the mountain. But the maidens were so fixed on looking back at their pursuers that they didn't see where they were going and fell into a lake. All were drowned and the lake is still known as Llyn y Morynion, 'The Lake of the Virgins'. Blodeuedd herself, however, did not meet this fate. To her pleading for mercy Gwydion said, 'I will not kill you. You came from Nature and to Nature you shall return. I shall transform you into a bird. But a bird that dares not show its face in daylight for fear of being mobbed by other birds. All for the shame you brought upon Lleu.' With a sweep of his wand Gwydion turned Blodeuedd into Blodeuwedd, the flower-faced owl. And so is the owl still called today.

Gronw Pebr was shocked to hear that the man he thought he'd killed was after him. He fled to Penllyn. When Lleu caught up with him, Gronw offered land and gold in recompense, but Lleu was not interested. 'You must stand in the same place I stood,' he said, 'and allow me to throw a spear at you.' Gronw tried to persuade one of his retinue to take the blow for him, but not one of them would. As a result they became 'One of the Three Disloyal Warbands of Britain'. So the two men went to the banks of the Cynfael river and Gronw stood where Lleu had been. At the last minute Gronw said, 'Since I acted through the deceit of a woman, please, in God's name, let me put that stone between me and the blow.' And Lleu said he could. So Gronw lifted a huge stone and crouched behind it. Then Lleu, the Fair One with the Deft Hand, took aim and threw the spear, straight as a beam of light. It seared through stone and flesh, bone and heart. Gronw Pebr, Gronw the Radiant, Lord of the Beasts and Wildman of the Woods, lay dead, killed by the Lord of Light. The stone with the hole lies there to this day and is known as Llech Gronw, Gronw's Stone.

As for Lleu he took back his lands and, according to the tale, after Math's death became Lord of Gwynedd and ruled over the country well. And so ends this branch of *The Mabinogion*.

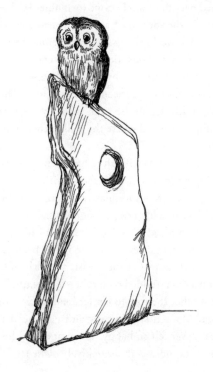

THE Emperor Dreams of Elen

The Emperor of Rome, Macsen Wledig, was out hunting with his nobles in a river valley to the north of his city. In the heat of the day the emperor grew sleepy, so his men tied up the dogs, erected a shelter of shields and Macsen lay down to rest. No sooner was he asleep than he began to dream.

In his dream he found himself floating up the river to its source high in the mountains. Over the snowy peaks he flew and beyond caught sight of a fertile plain with a wide river flowing north to the sea. At the mouth of the river was a fabulous city surrounding a castle with multi-coloured towers. Moored in the port was an immense fleet of ships. One of them, grander than the rest, had planks of silver and gold and a bridge to the shore of gleaming ivory. He crossed the bridge, a sail was raised and the ship skimmed over the sea. He came to another land with another splendid city at the mouth of another broad river. Over many miles of fair and fertile lowlands he travelled until he reached more steep and rugged mountains. Beyond these crags he saw an island separated from the mainland by a strait. At one end of the strait was a castle, the most magnificent he'd ever seen. The castle gate was open so, in his dream, he went through a golden door and entered an impressive hall where the walls were studded with glittering jewels.

Sitting on a golden couch before him were two tawny-headed youths playing gwyddbwyll (like chess) with golden pieces on a silver board. Both were immaculately dressed. Nearby, on a chair of ivory inlaid with golden eagles, sat a silver-haired man carving chess pieces from a rod of red gold. Next to him, on a golden throne, was a maiden, utterly dazzling in her beauty. She wore a shift of white silk clasped at the breast, a mantle of crimson brocaded silk and a tiara studded with rubies and pearls. The moment they saw each other she rose to her feet and reached out her arms towards him. Macsen strode over and embraced the maiden warmly. He'd never felt so happy. They sat down, he pressed his cheek against hers and was about to kiss her when …

A dog barked, sparking off the rest. Shields knocked against spears. Horses snorted and stamped. And the emperor … woke up! Emerging from the enchantment of his dream he was desolate. In an instant his joy turned to despair. He felt as if he'd lost everything. He could hardly stand. His nobles urged him to return to his palace to eat but he mounted his horse the saddest man alive. In the days that followed he lost interest in matters of state, in feasting and entertainment. All he wanted to do was sleep, hoping he might glimpse the maiden again. But when he awoke his life was still miserable and empty. Soon there were mutterings in his court. Something was wrong with the emperor. Complaints were sent up the chain of command. Finally Macsen realised he must do something. He summoned his wisest men and told them of his dream, concluding: 'Unless I see her soon I care not whether I live or die.' He was advised to send messengers seeking news of his dream maiden. They wandered the world a whole year but returned none the wiser. An advisor urged him to go hunting in the place where he'd had the dream. There he recognised the river as the one he'd followed in his vision. So thirteen messengers were sent to follow the dream's directions.

Sure enough, over the mountains they went – not so easily as the emperor had in his dream – and down the other side. Across the plain they followed the river to its mouth where they came to the great city, castle and fleet. In the biggest ship they crossed the sea to the Island of Britain. They lost no time in crossing the island, coming at last to the mountains of Eryri. 'This must be the rugged terrain our lord saw,' they said. From the other side of the range they saw Arfon and the Island of Môn. And there at one end of the Menai Strait was a magnificent castle. Just as in the emperor's dream, the gate was open. They went in and everything was as their lord had described: the two lads playing gwyddbwyll, the old man carving chess pieces and the dazzling maiden seated on her chair of red gold. The messengers approached her and went down on their knees. 'Oh empress of Rome,' they said, 'we bring you greetings from the emperor himself.' She could see by their badges that they were messengers from Rome but thought they were mocking her. They explained that the emperor had seen her in a dream and could not live without her. 'Would she come with them,' they asked, 'or should the emperor come here to make her his wife?'

'If it is I whom the emperor loves, let him come here to fetch me,' she replied.

And so the messengers made their way by night and day, exhausting many horses until at last they arrived in Rome and gave the emperor their welcome news. 'We know her name and

her lineage,' they said. 'She is called Elen and no maid was ever so fitted to be your empress. When we have received our reward we will guide you to her.' The emperor gathered his army and set out with the messengers as guides. They crossed the Alps and France and came over the water to Britain. There Macsen swiftly overcame the island's rulers and rode straight on to Arfon where he recognised the castle. Inside the hall he saw Cynan and Adeon playing gwyddbwyll and Eudaf, their father, carving the pieces. And then he saw Elen, the maiden of his dreams, dressed exactly as he had envisioned her. 'Empress of Rome,' he proclaimed. 'I greet thee!' She rose to meet him; he embraced her warmly, pressed his cheek to hers and had that long awaited kiss. Later that day they were wed.

Soon after Emperor Macsen gave the kingship of the Island of Britain to Eudaf, Elen's father. He built her three major strong-holds in Caernarfon, Carmarthen and Caerleon. On Elen's suggestion roads were built between these three major forts, roads which have since been known as Ffwrdd Elen Luyddog, the Roads of Elen of the Hosts.

Taliesin and the Birth of Inspiration

There was once a woman of witchy power called Ceridwen. She was married to Tegid the Bald and they lived on the banks of Llyn Tegid near where Bala is today. Between them they had two children: a girl, Creirwy, the most beautiful girl in all Wales, and a boy who, alas, as she was beautiful so he was ugly. Not only that, he was dim-witted as well, so much so that he was known as Afagddu, or Utter Darkness.

Ceridwen loved her son and knew that there would be no way ahead for him unless she used her magical powers. So she leafed through the book of Fferyllt until she came to a recipe for the Cauldron of Inspiration. 'That's what's my son needs,' she thought. 'If he's inspired he will be desired in the courts of the land, doesn't matter what he looks like.'

The recipe required many ingredients to be gathered at different times of the moon. From the seashore she scooped up an apron full of seaweed. On the high hills she scraped rare lichens into her magic pouch. In the woods she gathered mosses and charm-bearing herbs. From the meadows she brought baskets full of wildflowers. She even went into caves and mined for precious minerals. When all the ingredients were collected she placed them in a great cauldron, large enough for a man to sit inside. Then she checked the recipe to see how long it had to be brewed. To her dismay she found it was for a year and a day!

Ceridwen was modern in this respect. She was a busy woman. She couldn't hang around stirring the pot. So she employed the services of an old blind man called Morda who, because he was blind, had a helper, a guide boy, called Gwion Bach. As it turned out it was Gwion Bach ('the little fair-haired one') who did most of the work – gathering the firewood, feeding the fire and stirring the pot – while old Morda sat in his rocking chair, puffing on his pipe and occasionally muttering words of wisdom to the labouring lad.

And so the year passed. The buds of spring burst and blossom hung upon the trees. The birds sang and made their nests. The sun shone, the grasses grew, the crops ripened in the fields. People came with their scythes and sickles and gathered the harvest into the barns. Leaves on the trees turned gold and brown and the winds of autumn blasted them to the ground. And all through the long dark nights of winter, as the frost bit into Gwion Bach's ribs, he stirred and stirred.

At last the days began to lengthen, the buds began to swell. A whole year had passed. Ceridwen came to inspect the contents of the cauldron. By now it had bubbled down into a thick, black liquid. 'Aha!' she said. 'Soon it will be ready. I will have one more sleep and then I will be back.' She left Gwion Bach to stir for one last night. How his muscles ached, how his bones were weary, how he longed for the end of his labours.

Then, on the final morning, just as the sun was peeping over the horizon, three blessed drops flew from the cauldron and landed on Gwion Bach's finger. To cool his scalded finger he placed it in his mouth and, without realising what he was doing, swallowed the three drops down. Now it just so happened that all the inspiration intended for Afagddu was concentrated in those three drops. The rest was bitter poison. As he swallowed the drops a strange change came over him. He felt a tingle from the top of his head to the tip of his toes. Suddenly he was awake like never before. He blinked and looked up at the sky, and though the sun was rising he could see the shadows of the stars and he knew their names. In the fields the flowers nodded and smiled at him like old friends. He could remember back to the beginning of time and see into the future. And he knew that Ceridwen would be after him.

So he raced off down the mountainside and behind him the cauldron cracked into a dozen pieces. The bitter black liquid that remained oozed out of the pot, into a stream, down the hillside and later poisoned the horses of King Gwyddno as they drank. To this day that place is known as 'poisoned horses crossing'.

Ceridwen was woken by the cracking of the cauldron. She rushed to see what had happened. Instantly she knew and she was furious. All that hard work for her son Afagddu gone to Gwion Bach. You might think he deserved it but Ceridwen didn't see it like that. She was determined to punish the lad so she raced off down the mountainside after him.

Gwion Bach could sense her coming. Now not only did he know everything but he also had magical powers. So to escape from Ceridwen he thought 'hare' and instantly zigzagged off down the hillside. But she too had magical powers and turned herself into a hound. If there's one thing that can catch a hare it's a hound. The hound was about to nip the tail of the hare when it came to a river, leapt into the water and turned into a fish, a blue salmon, and went leaping upstream. But Ceridwen turned into a brown, silky otter and went swish, swish after the salmon. She was about to nip the tail of the salmon when it leapt into the air, sprouted wings and turned into a bird, a white dove. But she turned into a hawk, with a cruel hooked beak and sharp piercing eyes, and went straight as an arrow after that dove.

By now Gwion Bach was tiring of the chase. He looked down and saw far below a pile of winnowed wheat in a farmer's yard. He folded his wings and dropped like a stone from the sky. He was about to hit the ground when he transformed into a single golden grain and disappeared into the pile. But she turned into a black, red-crested hen and began scratching, squawking and pecking among the grains until at last she found the one that was Gwion Bach and she pecked it up and swallowed it down whole. And that, I'm afraid to say, was the end of Gwion Bach.

But not the end of the story.

Ceridwen became herself again and a few weeks later felt a quickening in her womb. She knew she was going to have a baby, and sure enough, nine months after swallowing the grain she gave birth to a baby boy. It was the most angelic child she had ever seen, but she knew it was Gwion Bach. All she wanted to do was to slit its throat. But you know what sweet, charming creatures babies are. You can't slit their throats. So she did the next worst thing. She stitched the baby into a leather bag, placed it in a small coracle, took it down to the river, pushed it through the rushes and watched as the current carried it away. And it floated all the way down to the sea.

There it washed back and forth in the tides for many moons, some say many years. And in all that time who knows how many waves that had rolled half-way round the world crashed over it; how many creatures rose up from the deeps and whispered secrets into its ears. But somehow in all that time the child survived.

Remember Gwyddno of the poisoned horses? He lived down in mid-Wales between where Machynlleth and Aberystwyth are today. At the mouth of a river running through his land he'd built a fish weir, a salmon trap. It always caught plenty of fish there and it was his custom, every Calan Mai, every May eve, to give the fish in that weir to one of his subjects as a special favour. But this year he'd decided to give the favour to his very own son, Elffin.

Now Elffin was a spendthrift and a wastrel. He'd gambled away his father's money and had a pile of debts. He was always being dragged home drunk. His father was fed up with him. He said, 'Look Elffin, tomorrow you can have the fish in that weir. Do something good with them or that's it. I shall disinherit you!' It's not good to be disinherited when your father is the king, so the next day Elffin went to the weir with one of his henchmen. There wasn't a single fish in it!

Then he looked again and saw in the swirling water an object snagged on a post. He thought it might be something of value – a chest of treasure or a cask of wine – so his henchman paddled out in a coracle and he returned with a leather bag. He placed it at Elffin's feet. Elffin drew his dagger, leaned over and slit open the bag. Out stepped a young boy. There was light shining from his brow.

'Taliesin!' gasped Elffin, meaning 'shining brow'.

'Taliesin it is,' said the boy.

'But who are you and what are you doing here?' asked the astonished Elffin.

'In all the time you have had this fish weir never was there such good fortune as tonight. I will be worth far more to you than three hundred salmon ever would. For though I am little I am gifted mightily.'

Elffin was amazed. He lost no time. He picked up the boy, put him on his saddle and rode like the wind back to his father's hall. He burst in through the great oaken doorway and strode up to his father, sitting on his throne.

'Well,' bellowed Gwyddno. 'Did you catch many fish?'

'I did better than that,' said Elffin. 'I caught a poet.'

'Pah!' spat Gwyddno. 'What use is that?'

'I will be worth far more to you than that fish weir ever was,' said the young Taliesin.

'What! You are able to speak and you so little?' gasped the dumbfounded Gwyddno.

'I am better able to speak than you are to question me,' said the boy.

At that a chastened Gwyddno simply replied, 'Well, in that case you'd better speak.'

And then it was that the young Taliesin spoke his first great poem:

I am Taliesin.

I make poetry of perfect metre and rhyme that will last
till the end of the world.

I know why breath is black, why silver gleams,
why liver is bloody.

I know why a cow has horns, why milk is white,
why a woman is affectionate.

I know why ale is bitter, why brine is salt;
why a kid is bearded, why cow parsley is hollow.

I know why the cuckoos complain,
where the cuckoos of summer are in winter.

I know what beasts there are at the bottom of the sea.

I know how many drops in a shower, how many spears in a battle,
Why a fish has scales, why a white swan has black feet.

I have been a blue salmon.

I have been a dog, a stag, a roebuck on the mountain;
A stock, a spade, an axe in the hand; a stallion, a bull, a buck.

A grain of wheat I grew on the hill.

I was reaped and placed in an oven.

I fell to the ground as I was being roasted.

A black hen swallowed me.

For nine nights I was in her crop.

I have been dead. I have been alive.

I am Taliesin.

So it was that the young Taliesin became Elffin's bard. And from that day onwards Elffin's fortune changed and he became happy and healthy, wealthy and wise. Well, at least until the day that he went to the court of Maelgwn Gwynedd and couldn't help boasting about his poet.

The Contention of the Bards

When Taliesin was 13 years old, Elffin was invited to a Christmas feast at the castle in Deganwy, the home of his uncle Maelgwn Gwynedd. As the feasting progressed the tipsy, well-fed bards toasted the king and sang his praises – that he was the most hand-some and generous king; that he had the fairest and most virtuous wife; that his bards were the wisest and cleverest of all. Elffin bit his lip and said nothing whilst the bootlicking bards uttered their grovelling compliments. But when he heard Maelgwn's bards claim they were the best, he could restrain himself no longer. 'No!' he shouted, springing to his feet. 'I have the wisest bard in the land.'

With this Maelgwn's face reddened. 'What!' he roared. 'How dare you claim anything of yours is better than mine. Into the dungeons with him.' And Elffin was unceremoniously dragged into the dark, damp dungeons where he was chained to the wall.

Taliesin, far away, knew what had happened. Swift as thought he made his way to the castle at Deganwy. As he travelled he sang to himself a poem which began:

> I will set out on foot,
> to the gate I will come,
> I will enter the hall,
> my song I will sing,
> my verse I will proclaim,
> and the king's bards I will cast down.
> In the presence of the Chief,
> demands I will make,
> and the chains I will break –
> Elffin will be set free.

When Taliesin arrived at Deganwy a feast was in progress. Once more the bards were about to sing in praise of Maelgwn. Taliesin slipped in through a side door and sat in a dark corner. When the court bards entered the unseen Taliesin pointed his finger at them, pouted his lips and flipped them with his forefinger. The sound he made has traditionally been written 'blerwm, blerwm …'

The gaggle of unwitting bards ostentatiously made their way to the front and cleared their throats. Everyone fell silent. Heinin, their chief, drew himself up to his full height and prepared to speak.

But when he opened his mouth what came out was: 'blerwm, blerwm!' No matter how hard he tried, that was the only sound he could make. It was the same with all the other bards. Maelgwn was furious and ordered one of his squires to strike Heinin. This broke his trance and he told his lord that the cause of his speechlessness was the spirit in the form of the youth who sat in the corner.

Maelgwn ordered the boy to be brought before him. 'Tell me who you are,' he demanded. Taliesin answered the king in verse, including such lines as:

Primary chief bard am I to Elffin, and my original country is the region of the summer stars. I know the names of the stars from north to south; I was in the court of Don before the birth of Gwydion. I have been loquacious prior to being gifted with speech; I have been three periods in the prison of Arianrhod; I am a wonder whose origin is not known. I have obtained the muse from the cauldron of Ceridwen; I have been fostered in the land of the Deity … I was for nine months in the womb of the hag Ceridwen; Originally I was little Gwion, and at length I am Taliesin.

The king and his nobles were amazed. They'd never heard anything like it from a boy so young. Maelgwn then ordered a riddling contest between the boy bard and Heinin to decide who was best. Immediately Taliesin began to speak:

Tell me then.
I was upon the Earth before God's flood
without flesh or vein or bone or blood.
Headless, footlessly I stride,
nothing's child, never born,
when my breath stills I am not dead.
No older now nor ever young
I have no need of beast or man.
Sea whitener, forest piercer,
handless, I touch a whole field.
Wide as the wide earth is wide.

Landless, invisible and blind,
gentle, murderous, without sin.
I am wet and dry and weak and strong.
What am I?

Whilst he still sang the doors rattled and the dogs whined as a
great storm swirled about the castle threatening to blow it away.
The wind had answered its own riddle. The king called for Elffin
to be brought from the dungeon and Taliesin sang another charm
to release the chains.

By now there was no doubt that the young Taliesin was indeed
the finest bard. After stunning the assembly with more extraordinary poems, Elffin and Taliesin were free to go.

The Druid Prince

The ancient Druids have always been mysterious. They kept no
written records, preferring to rely on memory and the oral tradition. We know they were the priests of the Celtic peoples but
much of what else we know was reported by their enemies and
may be distorted. But one fact seems indisputable. At the time of
the Roman invasion the Island of Mona was the headquarters of
the Druids. And it was these Druids who were fuelling the resistance to the invasion. The Roman generals realised that to succeed
in their conquest they had to crush the power of the Druids.
The Roman attack on Mona – reported by Tacitus – is the one and
only appearance the Druids make in the pages of history.

The discovery in 1986 of a 'body in the bog' at Lindow Moss
near Manchester led to an intriguing interpretation of the man's
death by Anne Ross and Don Robins in *The Life and Death of
a Druid Prince*. Drawing on archaeology, folklore and a foren-
sic examination of the body, they constructed an extraordinary
account of human sacrifice at a dark time for the Celts soon
after the massacre of the Druids and the rebellion of Boudicca.
Although this story can never be proven it is both plausible

and convincing. And harrowing. It casts a grim light on a shadowy world. It may not be 'the truth' but it is likely to contain some truth – as with many traditional stories. Here, then, is a rendering of their tale.

~

It was known in antiquity as Mona, the largest of the three main islands off the 'Island of the Mighty'. Now called Ynys Môn by the Welsh and Anglesey by the English, I shall simply call it Môn. Surrounded by the Irish Sea on three sides and separated from a mountainous mainland by a narrow but turbulent strait, it is well protected. But being at the maritime hub of the British Isles it is also accessible by sea. With its low hills and fertile soil it has long been the granary of Gwynedd, giving rise to its title of Mâm Cymru, Mother of Wales. It has been occupied for at least 5,000 years, having the highest concentration of Neolithic burial chambers anywhere in Britain. It has also, therefore, long had sacred associations. So – protected yet accessible, fertile and spacious, holy since time immemorial – little wonder it was the centre of Druidic training and power. Perhaps it was their presence that called forth another name: 'the Isle of the Glory of the Powerful Ones'.

In many cultures divine favour is beseeched by making offerings. These can be small and everyday – grain, flowers, holy water – or they can be of greater value – swords, shields, chariots, golden torcs. This was a central practice among the Druids. Offerings are like payments made in return for a benevolence which the giver hopes the god or goddess will grant. The bigger the ask, the bigger the offer. The most valuable thing that can be given is a human life. Then it's called sacrifice. The continental Celts were said, by their enemies, to have made large-scale human sacrifices, though little evidence has been found of it. It may have happened to a degree in Britain too.

Often offerings were thrown into lakes. One such lake – Llyn Cerrig Fach, the Lake of the Little Stones – is on Môn. It was discovered by chance when Valley Airport was being built during the Second World War. A chain found in the mud was used to pull out a truck that had become stuck. Later it was seen to be unusual and after examination archaeologists declared it to be a 2,000-year-old slave chain – iron hoops were fixed round the necks of five men chained together. Further excavation uncovered cauldron fragments, a decorated bronze plaque, chariot parts, bridle bits, swords, spears, a shield-boss, a sickle, two pairs of iron tongs and the remains of a large, curved horn. Some items appear to have been deliberately broken before being thrown into the water. Many had a military association and were deposited between the fourth century bc and about ad 60. A smaller group of non-martial ornaments were deposited after that until later in the second century. It is likely that these ritual offerings were overseen by Druid priests. But something changed around ad 60. The question is, what?

The Roman invasion of Britain in ad 43 had made steady progress but the legions were still being harried by the Silures under Caradog in South Wales and by the Ordivices in the north. Emperor Claudius had proscribed Druidism in Gaul in ad 54 but the edict did not extend to Britain, surprising perhaps as Druidism had originated and was strongest here. Perhaps Claudius decided that the Druids in Britain would be put to the sword. Early in ad 60, under the command of Suetonius Paulinus, Roman forces were marshalled for an attack on Môn. Tacitus, whose father-in-law had been present on the day, takes up the story:

> Paulinus prepared to attack Mona which was very populous and a haven for refugees. He constructed a flotilla of flat-bottomed boats by which means the infantry crossed the variable channel. The cavalry did so by swimming at the side of their horses. On the beach stood a serried mass of arms and men, with women flitting between the ranks. Like the Furies, in robes of deathly black and with disheveled hair, they brandished their torches; while a circle of Druids, lifting their hands to heaven and showering curses, struck the troops with such an awe at the extraordinary spectacle that, as though their limbs were paralyzed, they exposed their bodies to wounds without an attempt at movement. Then, reproached by their general, and urging each other not to flinch before a band of

females and fanatics, they charged behind the standards, cut down all who met them, and enveloped the enemy in his own flames. The next step was to install a garrison among the conquered population and to demolish their consecrated groves.

Tacitus Annals XIV.xxix-xxx

But as Suetonius raised the victory cup to his lips it was dashed to the ground by the arrival of a messenger who'd ridden hotfoot from the south. The whole of the province was in flames. Prasutagus, King of the Iceni, had died. Catus, the Imperial Procurator, wanted all of his rich estate rather than the half he'd been offered. Boudicca, Queen of the Iceni, resisted. She was flogged and her daughters raped. She vowed bloody vengeance and was now leading the revolt. The Roman city of Colchester had been razed to the ground and the inhabitants slaughtered. Boudicca's army was now heading for London. To Paulinus it must have seemed like the fulfillment of the Druids' curses hurled at him only hours before. He set off with his cavalry down Watling Street towards London, ordering his two legions of infantry to follow behind. Instead of going to London, Boudicca's host turned north to meet the Ninth Legion who were hurrying south. Whether by dint of tactics or sheer numbers, Boudicca's forces were victorious and the Ninth Legion was wiped out. Returning south they burned London to the ground, then, on their way back north, levelled the Roman town of Verulanium, St Albans. At this moment there was a chance that the Roman advance in Britain could have been halted for good. But Suetonius Paulinus was a wily commander. He'd taken a big gamble and suffered huge losses. He put his military judgement to the ultimate test by choosing his battleground carefully. It was a narrow valley with protected flanks and a steep approach. By then the Britons must have been somewhat disorderly. Maybe some were sufficiently slaked in blood and wanted to get back to their fields. Though they vastly outnumbered the Romans, after their initial charge the battle turned into a rout. Boudicca fled from the battlefield and took poison. The Romans were merciless in their revenge.

So in early ad 60 the Britons suffered three terrible disasters. The Druids were shattered and their sacred groves cut down. Boudicca was dead along with (Tacitus tells us) 80,000 of her people. And, because of all the unrest (Tacitus again), farmers had abandoned planting the spring crops. There would be no harvest. It was the darkest hour. Nothing now, it seemed, could stop the Roman advance – even to Ireland, *insula sacra*, the most sacred island of all. The only thing that could be done was to beseech the vengeful gods and make the highest sacrifice. But who was going to make it, how and where?

Tara was a sacred centre in Ireland. It was there that the chosen children were brought for their long training. If successful they'd be in their late twenties before becoming fully initiated Druids. Their education began with tutoring the mind, developing both memory and powers of concentration. Ancestral lineages, the people's history, poetry and story were learned by heart for oral recitation. Students were introduced to the natural world, the seasonal cycles, the movements of the sun, moon, planets and stars. They mastered the wisdom of riddles. They learned the healing properties of herbs and the magical uses of mistletoe. They practised prophecying the future by reading the omens – in the flight of birds, later in the intestines of sacrificed creatures. They became familiar with chanting spells for calming the elements, inducing sleep and bringing victory in battle. They learned the law so they could settle disputes, determine succession and deal out punishments. They memorised the names of the gods and goddesses, their realms of power, how they could be communed with and propitiated. They learned the art of offering and sacrifice. They came to know and understand the immortal soul which could be reborn many times. And they learned how to face death without fear.

Toward the end of this process, after their final initiation rituals, they were each given a sacred name. One initiate was named for the fox, Lovernios. It was as a boy of 12 that he'd first heard of the Romans landing on the southern shores of Britain. Unlike before they looked intent on staying. But he was too busy with his education to worry about it much. Besides they were far away, beyond the sea and over the mountains. Lovernios was a bright and athletic student. He was also specially privileged, as his father was the king. When he reached his late twenties he was the pre-eminent graduate of his school and a natural leader. By this time the Roman clamour, though still distant, had become more trou-bling. Then suddenly one spring they were at the door. News came that two Roman legions were heading for beloved Môn intent on destroying Druid power. This was just across the water, 60 miles maybe, but not much of an obstacle to determined and ruthless Romans. Something had to be done.

Lovernios decided to act. He gathered around him a group of experienced Druids and an armed guard. It was a day's journey across the waters in a sea-sturdy currach. They arrived at nightfall on the Holy Island. Immediately they heard. The news was des-perate. Two legions had crossed the strait, slaughtered the priests, cut down the sacred groves. This was hard to bear. Lovernios had known some of those who now lay dead. At least the Romans had already left, which was a relief. They'd sped back south to confront Boudicca's Iceni uprising. Lovernios muttered a prayer of thanks and good wishes to Boudicca. In the morning he and his entou-rage made their way to the Lake of Offerings. He'd been here once before and taken part in a ceremony where a sword had been given to the lake spirits. But this occasion called for more, much more. This time he took off his golden torc – given to him to honour his special role as a Druid prince – and fingered it lovingly. Then with the appropriate incantations he carefully threw it into the holy waters. He sat a long time meditating and chanting, praying for courage and guidance. Then it came to him. The gods needed a greater gift, an offering that would surpass all others. To keep the Romans from crossing the sea to the *insula sacra* they needed to make the ultimate sacrifice. The question was, who would it be? And where? This place was not right. Too far away. It needed to be closer to the heart of things and yet in a spot where they wouldn't be disturbed. He consulted his colleagues and they told him of an area between the Roman frontline and their allies to the north which was still a no-man's-land. It was almost under the enemy noses yet hidden. There was a sacred grove there too. They climbed back into the currach and sailed in the dark along the northern coast of Cambria to the mouth of the Dee river. There they made landfall.

On the journey no one spoke about what they were going to do. But by the time they were walking inland towards the hill Lovernios knew. It would have to be him. He was the most high born. He was fit, healthy and the right age. He knew in a quietly proud way that he was a perfect gift for the gods. They wouldn't get any better than him. He had completed his education and he knew how these things worked. Yet it wasn't just about training. He was wise beyond his years. And he had no fear of death. This thing was too big to be afraid just for himself.

They reached the foot of the hill the day before Beltane eve. The woods were exploding with life around them. Lovernios drank it in – the delicate opening buds, the bluebells and blossoms, the singing birds. How bittersweet that this should be his last time, in this lifetime at least. That evening he sat with the other Druids and they discussed in detail the deed they were about to perform. No one had ever done anything like this before. Strangely it was Lovernios himself who led them through it. For this act to have maximum power it would have to be a triple sacrifice – to Taranis, god of the heavens, Esus, god of the earth and Teutates, god of the waters. Three blows on the head for the thunder god; garroting

and blood-letting for the lord of the lands; drowning in a dark pool, a llyn ddu, for the god of the people. He made sure they had everything necessary – ground barley to make the bannock, the club, the knife and the knotted cord made of fox sinew. Someone was sent to locate the dark pool a mile or two away from the hill. Someone else found a white horse. That night Lovernios walked up the hill and into the grove alone. From his pouch he took a few grains of mistletoe pollen and put them on his tongue. He let them rest there and slowly soften. He knew they would give him strength. He spent much of the night meditating on his task.

The morning came. Lovernios was breathing deeply now, noticing the pulsing of his heart. He watched a flower open, observed birds in flight. In the late afternoon someone prepared the bannock. Soon it would be time. As the sun touched the horizon one of the Druids spoke an invocation. Together they chanted. The bannock was taken from the small fire and broken into equal pieces, one for each person present. One portion was burned. Lovernios had explained that this would be for him. He picked it up, took a bite and chewed. The charcoal was bitter. There was more chanting. When it came to a natural end he rose to his feet and took off his clothes. From a pouch he pulled a band of fox fur and slid it on to his upper arm. Naked now but for fox. All the other men stood up and made a circle around him. He took some deep breaths and began stamping his feet rhythmically. As if from the Otherworld a voice came through him:

> I am Fox. I come from the earth. Strong I am, clever I am, beautiful I am. I run through the forest and catch my prey. I am oak and river and grass. I am sun and moon and stars. I come from the ancestors back to the beginning. I speak for my people across land and sea. I give myself as the greatest gift. To Taranis, to Esus, to Teutates. Let me die that we may live. Let me die that we may prevail. Let me die that the enemy halt. I live. I die. I give my life …

Two priests then took Lovernios by the arms into the centre of the grove where they kissed him, one on each cheek. He knelt, looking straight ahead. They were all chanting now. The blows came quickly and he was down and unconscious. Two of them held his limp body up while a third tied the cord round his neck, inserted a stick then tightened it with a few strangling twists. Lovernios was truly gone now. A fourth man pierced the artery with precision; another caught the gushing blood in a small cauldron. It was all over in a matter of minutes. Now the white horse was brought from the shadows. It was pulling a chariot. Fox's body was gently lifted on to it, together with an image of Anu, the great mother goddess. By the light of flaming torches the procession slowly made its way down a track from the sacred wooded hill to edge of the black pool, Llyn Ddu, Lindow. The body was lifted from the bier and, with final blessings reaching a crescendo in the mouths of the celebrants, was tipped into the peaty pool. The sacrifice was complete. The highest possible offering had been given to the gods of sky, water and earth in the company of the great mother.

And the Romans never did get to Ireland.

LEGENDS OF ARTHUR

Merlin, Dragons and Prophecy

Dinas Emrys

The mountains of Eryri are entered from the north by the valleys of Conwy, Ogwen and Peris and from the south by the valleys of Glaslyn, Waunfawr and Nantlle. All valleys more or less meet in one long north–south valley running through the centre of the mountains east of Yr Wyddfa called Gwynant. In that central valley, just north of Beddgelert, is a hill. At first sight it's nothing special. You could easily drive past it without noticing. Many do. But look again and you'll see a steep-sided, dome-shaped hill covered in oak trees that looks, from some angles, like a pregnant belly. More than 2,000 years ago it was a hill fort and the remnants of a rampart still encircle the hilltop.

Away from the road is a narrow neck of land which provides a way to the summit of this otherwise impregnable fortress. The path goes through a cleft in the rock, a natural gateway that could have been guarded by three men. At the top are the ruins of an old square tower, dated by archaeologists to about the twelfth century. Just below this structure is a hidden, bowl-shaped valley. It is a valley in a hill in a valley in the hills. On one side the bowl dips down into a gully where the water from a rush-choked pool trickles over the edge before disappearing underground. This hidden valley in the pregnant-belly-shaped hill is rather like a womb. According to legend it is indeed a place that gave birth – to dragons.

The hill is Dinas Emrys, meaning the stronghold of the divine or the immortal. For at least 1,500 years it is likely to have been a gathering place for the Brythonic tribes of North Wales, perhaps for the whole of Wales. Whenever danger threatened – and it happened many times – the chieftains and spiritual guides of these ancient native peoples retreated to this heart of the heartland to take council with each other. In this natural amphitheatre they gave and received guidance and invited prophetic inspiration. For this place was an Omphalos, a Sacred Centre around which a people once revolved and to which they once came to strengthen their resolve. It was here that King Lludd is said to have buried two dragons which had been causing a disturbance at the centre of the land. And it was here, after the Romans had left and when the Saxons were invading, that the dragons once again stirred. It was here, too, that a boy was brought – a child of destiny – who uttered a prophecy remembered to this day.

Merlin and the Dragons

The earliest version of this story was written by Nennius in the ninth century in *Historia Brittonum*. In 1136 Geoffrey of Monmouth expanded the tale in *The History of the Kings of Britain*. Two hundred copies of this book were made by hand and within ten years were to be found in all the capital cities of Europe. Purporting to tell nearly 2,000 years of British history it was the first 'bestseller' of all time after the Bible. The last quarter was devoted to the stories of Merlin and Arthur. The book was to be a major influence on European culture over the next two centuries.

The story concerning Dinas Emrys begins after the Romans had left Britain. A period of chaos ensued, though there was a rightful king called Constantine who had two sons, Ambrosius and Uther. He also had a 'prime minister' known as 'Vortigern the Thin'. However, Vortigern coveted the crown for himself and so arranged for a visiting band of Picts to assassinate the king. The king's sons were whisked off to Brittany for safekeeping. At the time Britain was being attacked by the Picts from the north and the Saxons from the east. So Vortigern invited in Saxon mercenaries to fend off the Picts. They were good fighters and the Picts were sent packing.

In payment for their efforts, Vortigern gave the Saxons the green, fertile, well-watered lands of Kent, still known as the Garden of England. And Vortigern was given Rowena, the daughter of the Saxon leader, as his wife. For the usurper king it proved a fatal move.

The Saxons came pouring in. Soon Kent wasn't enough. They wanted more. So they sent a message to Vortigern demanding a meeting to discuss land and peace. The meeting was held on the Salisbury plain. A great tent was erected. Because it was to be a meeting about peace, all weapons were laid on the ground outside. They sat in a circle, British chieftains next to Saxon chieftains. Hengist, the Saxon leader, said it would improve relations between them. Vortigern rose to his feet and made a speech. Then it was Hengist's turn. But at a pre-arranged moment he cried out: 'Nimet ver saxes!' – 'Out with your knives' – and the Saxon chieftains reached into their boots, pulled out long knives and plunged them mercilessly into the hearts of the British chieftains sitting next to them. It was a dastardly deed and became known as 'the treachery of the long knives'.

Miraculously, Vortigern escaped. He tipped over the table, grabbed a knife, ripped a hole in the tent, leapt on to a horse and, with a handful of his men, galloped away. When they had thrown their pursuers he asked: 'Where shall we go?' The advice came back: 'Head for the mountains of Eryri. There we can find refuge.' So they rode to Gwynedd and, beneath the looming summit of Yr Wyddfa, came upon a hill. They tethered their horses and Vortigern sent a scout to investigate. He came back with encouraging news so they set up camp and a few days later carpenters and stonemasons began building a tower. But a strange thing happened. Every morning on returning to their work they found their previous day's efforts fallen to the ground. This happened for three days. Finally Vortigern consulted an old Druid who examined the omens and oracles and said that Vortigern must find a fatherless boy and spill his blood on the ground. Only then, he said, would the walls stand firm.

Not knowing what else to do Vortigern sent messengers throughout the land looking for a fatherless boy. They came, at length, to Caerfyrddin in South Wales. They were resting outside the town walls idly gossiping when they noticed a group of youths playing football. Suddenly a quarrel erupted among the lads. It seemed they were all picking on one boy. Then one voice rose above the others. 'Well we don't even know who you are! You don't even have a father!' The messengers nudged each other, marched up to the boy, clapped a hand on his shoulder and said: 'Boy, take us to your mother!'

The boy's mother was, according to Geoffrey of Monmouth, a nun from a nearby convent. She claimed that she didn't know the boy's father as she'd been visited in the night by an incubus, a demonic spirit. This, she'd discovered, was a convenient story approved by the priests of Iesu Grist. But there is another possibility that may be closer to the truth. Perhaps the boy's mother was a princess and priestess of the Old Faith. In that remote corner of Britain it was still strong. There the Druids and priestesses had divined that the extremity of the times demanded the ritual conception of a child of destiny, a child who would become a great teacher and a saviour of his age. She had been chosen by the Goddess for her purity, perfection and wisdom to take part in this Great Rite. On the appointed night she'd walked willingly along the dark, lonely path to the sacred grove. As the wind sighed through the trees, she waited by the firelight. From the shadows stepped a figure. She would never know his name for his face was masked. It was enough for her that he had been chosen by the Goddess. They moved together into the age-old dance and that night the child of destiny was conceived.

At birth the child was welcomed according to the old traditions, but he was also baptised into the new religion so that he could walk between the two worlds. But when the Christian priests found out what had happened they were horrified. They put about a story that the Devil had sent an incubus to impregnate an innocent maiden so that he could have a servant on Earth. What good fortune, they said, that the child was baptised, thus thwarting the Devil's plan. In time the child's mother found this to be a convenient way to explain why she couldn't name the father.

So the soldiers bundled the boy on to a horse and rode with him back up to the mountains. They dismounted, dragged him through the cleft in the rock and were just approaching Vortigern's tumbled tower, with the sacrificial priest sharpening his knife, when the boy escaped from his captors. He leapt on to a rock and cried out: 'No! This talk of sacrifice is nothing but lies. I will tell you why your walls fail to stand.' For this boy was none other than the young Merlin, and he had the Sight. He could see things other people couldn't see.

'If you dig here you will find an underground pool. Drain that pool and you'll find two stone jars. And in those jars … No, wait. Dig now and prove me wrong!'

Vortigern was impressed by the courage and confidence of the boy and ordered his soldiers to dig. Soon the earth was flying through the air and sure enough they came to an underground pool. They drained the pool and there in a dripping cavern spied the two great stone jars. They were just approaching them when the jars

cracked open like giant eggs hatching and out emerged two fledg-
ling dragons, a fire dragon and an ice dragon. They crawled out of
their dingy dungeon into the light and, like butterflies emerging
from a cocoon, dried their wings in the sun. Then they grew back
into their full size and finally caught sight of each other once more.
At that moment they resumed their eternal combat, rising up on
their leathery wings, chasing each other back and forth across the
sky until finally the red dragon drove the white dragon over the
horizon, leaving Vortigern and his men trembling with fear. 'But
what does it mean?' he stammered, 'What does it mean?'

Then it was that the young Merlin spoke his first great prophecy.
He inhaled the breath of prophecy, burst into tears and uttered
these words:

The Dragon's are awake,
there is a disturbance in the Land.
The white dragon is the Saxon invader,
the greedy, grasping newcomer.
The red dragon is the people of Britain, the bearers of tradition,
those who have been here since the beginning.
They will chase each other back and forth across this land
until such a time as arises the Boar of Cornwall.
Only then will peace and harmony be restored.
He will be the noblest king,
and tales of his exploits will be as meat and drink
to the storytellers who relate them in ages to come.

But chaos will return
and there will be centuries of destruction
until a people in wood and iron coats
come and restore the ancient ones to their homes.
The eagle shall build its nest on Mount Yr Wyddfa.
Gold shall be squeezed from the lily and the nettle,
silver shall flow from the hooves of bellowing cattle.
From the first to the fourth, the fourth to the third,
the third to the second the thumb shall roll in oil.

Though the Goddess be forgotten
there will come a time of plenty
when the soil will be fruitful beyond man's need.
The Fatted Boar will proffer food and drink;
the Hedgehog will hide his apples in London.
Underground passages will be built beneath the city.
Stones will speak; the sea to France will shrink
and the secrets of the deep will be revealed.

But beware the Ass of Complacency,
swift against goldsmiths, slow against ravenous wolves.
Oak trees shall burn and acorns grow on lime trees.
The Severn river will flow out through seven mouths.
Fish will die in the heat and from them serpents will be born.
And the health giving waters at Bath shall breed death

Then root and branch shall change place,
And the newness of the thing shall seem a miracle.
The healing maiden will return, her footsteps bursting into flame.
She will weep tears of compassion for the people of the land,
Dry up polluted rivers with her breath,
Carry the forest in her right hand, the city in her left,
And nourish the creatures of the deep.

With her blessing
Man will become like God
Waking as if from a dream:
Heart open and filled with light,
Radiant face, glowing like the rising sun,
Shining eyes, like twin silver moons,
Radiant ears, shimmering with song,
Shining lips, that dance over words,
Words of magic that burst into the air becoming swallows.
The soul shall walk out; the mind of fire shall burn.
And, in the twinkling of an eye, the dust of the ancients
Shall be restored.

The young Merlin collapsed to the ground, exhausted from the effort of prophecy. When he came to, Vortigern was looming over him: 'But what about me?' he wanted to know. '

All you can do is flee for your life,' replied Merlin.

And so it was that Vortigern fled with the rump of his supporters further to the west. On the Llŷn Peninsula he took a steep path down to a hidden valley by the sea. There he built a timber tower and lived in uneasy peace for some months. But Ambrosius and Uther had now come of age. They returned from Brittany to claim their rightful inheritance. They knew the first thing they must do was deal with Vortigern so they tracked him down through Eryri to his hiding place. There, with a single flaming arrow, they set fire to his tower. Once again Vortigern was forced to flee for his life. He ran along the beach and up on to the clifftop. His pursuers were closing in on him. He took one last breath and leapt to his death on the rocks far below. That place is still known as the Rock of the Leap and the valley is called Nant Gwytheryn, or the Valley of Vortigern. Ever after Vortigern was remembered as one of the 'Three Dishonoured Men who were in the Island of Britain'.

As for Merlin, he knew that from that moment onwards it would be his task to bring about the rise of the Boar of Cornwall, who was none other than Arthur himself.

Many Merlins

Although that is the most well known story about Merlin, no single tale can encompass the myriad guises in which he is found. Geoffrey of Monmouth, responsible for launching him as a character into the world, gave two rather different versions of his life. In *The History of the Kings of Britain* Merlin was the prophet who foresaw the coming of Arthur, brought about his conception and then became his chief counsellor. But in *The Life of Merlin*, written later, after his lord Gwendolau was slain in the Battle of Arderydd in ad 573 (one of the 'Three Futile Battles of the Island of Britain'), Merlin went mad with grief and became a wildman living like an animal in the forest. After much lamenting he drank from a healing spring and recovered his senses. This suggests there may have been more than one Merlin, or at least that Merlin lived out many roles over his life, from wildman, shape-changer and lord of the beasts to prophet, high priest and adviser to kings.

One of the oldest surviving fragments of story about Merlin (in the *White Book of Rhydderch*) says that 'before it was taken or settled these islands were known as Clas Myrddin', which means Merlin's sacred precinct or enclosure. So it could be that 'the Merlin' was the high priest of Britain, guiding and protecting the people over generations. Perhaps he was the one who anointed kings and symbolically wed them to Sovereignty, the Goddess of the Land. There are even hints that he may have been the chief architect of that great temple of Neolithic Britain, Stonehenge.

What became of Merlin? Well, according to the stories he did not die. Rather, like the old pagan faith itself, he went underground, back to the land, enfolded in the arms of the Goddess. Some say he was ensnared with a spell by his lover Nimue, trapped beneath a rock or within a blossoming hawthorn tree. Others say that he went to a house of glass on an island to the west. For the rest of that story see 'Merlin, Bardsey and the Thirteen Treasures' below.

The Ancient Animals

A folk tale, collected on Anglesey by P.H. Emerson and published in *Welsh Fairy-Tales and Other Stories* (1894), tells of Eagle, whose wife has died and offspring have left home. He decides to find a new wife, but wants one who is old and wise. He is keen on Owl but, to be sure she's truly old, asks Stag, Salmon, Blackbird and Frog. They all confirm that, despite their great age, they've never known Owl to be younger than she is now. She is older than old so Eagle is satisfied and the pair are wed.

It's a sweet tale, devised perhaps for children. But the original story, found in 'Culhwch and Olwen' in *The Mabinogion*, is a stronger and more mysterious tale. Like the theme of the story, it seems like a remnant of something very old – from a time when animals were imbued with sacred powers. Maybe its roots go back even beyond the Neolithic to the days when hunter-gatherers roamed these lands. It is likely that the locations in the story involving Eagle and Owl were in Snowdonia. Also Mabon, son of Modron, a key figure in this story, is said, in 'The Stanzas of the Graves', to be buried in the upper Nantlle Valley. The probable location, near Llyn Nantlle, is now under a huge slate tip. It is possible that, rather than being buried there, it is the place people come to invoke Mabon's spirit. Either way it is a good reason to include the story about Mabon in this collection. So here is a very abridged version of 'Culhwch and Olwen', the earliest story to feature Arthur.

❦

His stepmother had cursed Culhwch to marry no other woman but Olwen, daughter of Ysbaddaden, the Chief Giant. Though all her previous suitors had perished at the hands of her father (whose death was prophecied on the day his daughter married), Olwen's name inflamed Culhwch with passionate desire. Culhwch's father suggested he go to his cousin Arthur's court to seek help.

Culhwch rode on a fine grey steed with sturdy shoulders and hooves like shells. Its bit was of gold; its saddle was inlaid with gold. In one hand he carried two silver spears, in the other a great battleaxe so sharp it could draw blood from the wind. And on his thigh he wore a golden sword that glinted in the morning sunlight. In front ran his two white greyhounds criss-crossing from one side to the other, as four clods of earth from the horse's hooves flew about his ears like swallows …

The Gatekeeper refused him entry into Arthur's hall, so he issued a threat. 'If you do not open the gate,' he said, 'I will let out such a cry that it will be heard from Penwith in Cornwall to the Cold Ridge in Ireland and Dinsol in the far north. What is more, every woman who hears it will be so frightened she will fall barren and never bear children again!' After consulting Arthur, the Gatekeeper let him in and, still trotting on his horse, he rode into the great hall.

Culhwch was given six of Arthur's best men (including Cai and Bedwyr) and granted permission to seek Olwen. It was a job and a half to find her, but that was just the start of it. She – dressed in a robe of flame-red silk with hair yellower than the flower of the broom and breasts whiter than the breasts of a swan – was every-thing Culhwch imagined she would be. He wanted her at once but she said he must first get her father's permission, which would not be easy. It wasn't easy. Ysbaddaden kept trying to impale them with a poisoned iron spear. When that failed he grudgingly listened and then presented thirty-nine impossible tasks for Culhwch to accom-plish. Unattainable though they sounded, after each one Culhwch tossed his head contemptuously and retorted: 'Ha! That's easy. Next!'

For the wedding Ysbaddaden required his haystack hair be cut and his thorny thicket of a beard be shaved. There was only one pair of scis-sors, one razor and one comb powerful enough to do this barbering job and they were between the ears of Twrch Trwyth, the most savage wild boar in the land. So one of the nigh-on impossible tasks was to get these tools from The Boar, who would not willingly give them up. There was only one horse which could catch The Boar, and that was the white horse with the dark mane. And there was only one man able to ride that horse and that was Mabon, son of Modron (the Great Son of the Great Mother). But he'd been taken from his mother when he was only three days old and no one had seen him since.

So they had to find Mabon, son of Modron. Arthur suggested they ask the Ancient Animals to help. His warriors hesitated, thinking it was below them to talk to animals, but Arthur insisted. First Culhwch and his companions came to the Blackbird of Cilgwri. Gwrhyr, the Interpreter of Tongues (who could speak all human and animal languages), said: 'We are Arthur's messengers seeking Mabon, son of Modron. Have you ever heard of him?' The Blackbird said: 'I am old, very old. When I was young there was a great iron anvil here and every night I've wiped my beak on it. Now it's no bigger than a nut. But in all that time I've never heard of the man you seek. However, there is one older than I and that is the Stag of Rhedynfre. Go to speak to the Stag.'

They went to Rhedynfre and Gwrhyr said: 'We are Arthur's messengers, seeking Mabon, son of Modron. Do you know of him?' The Stag said: 'I am old, very old. When I was young there was an oak sapling here. It grew into a great tree with 100 branches. Then it withered with age and fell. Now all that's left is this red stump. But in all that time I've never heard of the man you seek. However, there is one older than I and that is the Owl of Cwm Cawlwyd. Go to speak to the Owl.'

So they went to Cwm Cawlwyd and Gwrhyr made his speech. The Owl said: 'I am old, very old. When I was young a great forest filled this valley. Then a race of men came – men who live such a short time – and they cut down the trees. But the trees grew back and the forest you see before you now is the third forest to fill this valley. But in all that time I've never heard of the man you seek. However, there is one older than I and that is the Eagle of Gwernabwy. Go to speak to the Eagle.'

They went to Gwernabwy and Gwrhyr asked once more about Mabon. The Eagle said: 'I am old, very old. When I was young there was a great rocky crag here. Every night I would stand on top of that crag and peck at the stars. Now that rock is no bigger than a fist. But in all that time never have I heard of the man you seek. However … once I went to the pool at Llyn Llyw and there I saw a mighty fish. It would feed me for many days. So I flew down and sank my talons into its back. But it pulled me under the water. It was all I could do to escape. Later I went with my kinsmen to make war on that Salmon but the Salmon offered us only peace. I drew fifty barbs from the back of that fish. If the Salmon doesn't know about the man you seek I don't know who will.'

So they went to Llyn Llyw and Gwrhyr asked again. 'What I know I will tell,' said the Salmon. 'Every tide I swim up the Severn river to the sea fortress of Caer Loyw (Gloucester) where I hear the worst lamenting I've heard since the beginning of time. There I believe you'll find the man you seek.' So Cai and Gwrhyr mounted the shoulders of the Salmon and they swam up the Severn river to Caer Loyw where they heard the terrible wail.

'Who is there?' cried Gwrhyr.

'It is I, Mabon, son of Modron,' a voice came back.

'How may we free you, by barter or by battle?'

'It is only by battle I may be freed.'

And so Cai scaled the battlements, Gwrhyr summoned Arthur's warriors and in the fierce fighting that followed Mabon – one of the 'Three Exalted Prisoners of the Island of Britain' – was set free.

The hunt for Twrch Trwyth was bitter and bloody. Many of Arthur's finest men, horses and dogs were slain. But at last, on the banks of the Severn river, Mabon, son of Modron, riding on the white horse with the dark mane, swooped down and plucked the scissors, razor and comb from between the ears of the wild boar.

After all the many other tasks were accomplished, Ysbaddaden's haystack hair was cut and his thorny thicket of a beard was shaved. Culhwch asked the giant: 'Ysbaddaden, art thou shaved?' And he replied: 'I am shaved. But you never would have achieved this without Arthur's help. And now I must give up my life.' And so he was taken into the courtyard and his great head was cut from his body. It was placed on a post high on the battlements and there was great relief and rejoicing.

Culhwch and Olwen were wed and the celebrations went on for a month and a day. They lived happily to the end of their lives. As for Mabon, I like to think he is alive to this day, hunting and helping people in need. But if you want to find him you'll have to ask … the Salmon.

Rhitta and the Cloak of Beards

It was a grand boast. Nyniaw and Peibiaw, brothers and somewhat lesser kings, were prone to locking horns and winding each other up something rotten. They should have known it would end in tears. In fact it was worse than that. It ended up, according to Ysbaddaden the Chief Giant, with them being transformed for their sins into oxen, bitter beasts of burden. But at the time of the story they were young and foolish, carried away, perhaps, by the glory of a starlit summer's night.

'Look up brother,' said Nyniaw, 'and gaze upon my wide and wondrous field, the most extensive pasture in the whole world!'

'What are you talking about?' frowned Peibiaw.

'Why the sky of course. It's my meadow. As far as the eye can see, all mine!'

'Huh, it may be,' shot back Peibiaw, quick as a wink, 'but those are my countless herds of cattle and flocks of sheep grazing in your field.'

Nyniaw was affronted. 'What do you mean?' he said.

'The stars,' said Peibiaw, 'each sparkling one of them mine, tended most lovingly by my lady the Moon.'

'You shall not graze your animals in my field!' shouted Nyniaw.

'Oh I can and I shall,' taunted Peibiaw.

They were back in the playground: 'Can!' 'Can't!' 'Shall!' 'Shan't!' This is how it goes. Shouts led to blows, blows led to combat and combat led to battle, full-scale bloody death and destruction. Both kingdoms were utterly devastated. All over who owned the grazing rights in Heaven.

Now the somewhat bigger king at the time was Rhitta. He was a man and a half. In fact he was more like two men, twice the size of any other. No wonder he was known as a giant. When he heard about the deadly squabble between Nyniaw and Peibiaw he thought he'd better put a stop to it. After all, if anyone owned the celestial sward it was him. So he swiftly marched to where they were licking their wounds, scooped them up by the scruffs of their necks and banged their heads together. 'Let that be a lesson to you,' he said. But then he had a better idea. Their beards! They were sporting a pair of rather fine beards. He promptly had them cut off and stitched into a rather fetching cap.

Were they merely shaved or rather more brutally flayed? The bards of old did not say.

When news of this insult to royal beards got around, the other twenty-eight kings of Britain were outraged. Determined to punish Rhitta they marched to his stronghold, intent on putting him to the sword. It was an impressive show of unity, rare in such dark and desparate days. But Rhitta was not easily overcome. Indeed he fell upon this crisis of kings like the first gale of autumn, vanquishing them all thoroughly. It was an impressive display of brute strength. Having now developed an appetite for sewing beards, he commanded that all the defeated kings be stripped of their whiskers and that these then be sewed into a cloak. Work began at once on this hairy mantle.

But peace was not yet won. Word of the assault on beards spread beyond the island's shores to neighbouring lands. Yet more keenly affronted kings mustered armies against Rhitta, all in fear for their beards. And all to no avail. Rhitta was once again victorious and a further swathe of beards were shaved or flayed. They were all stitched into his mighty cloak, which now stretched from head to heel and kept him warm at night whenever he went out to inspect his celestial sheep. It was a magnificent garment and Rhitta was rightly proud.

One day, however, Rhitta realised that there was a gap at the bottom of his marvellous mantle. He needed one more beard to fill it. It was on that same day that he heard of Arthur, a young king in the south who Rhitta had yet to overcome and whose beard, he thought, would finish off the cloak perfectly. So he sent a messenger offering Arthur the simple option of flaying his own beard and sending it to him. For once he thought it might save on bloodshed.

Arthur was washing his hands after slaying a red-eyed Cornish giant when Rhitta's messenger arrived. He listened quietly to the request and then said that he was still young and that his own beard was too meagre for such a patching job. However, if Rhitta insisted on pursuing the matter he would engage himself to find

a beard suited for the purpose. Yet he advised him to rest content with what he had. Rhitta, however, would not rest content and sent a message to Arthur challenging him to a duel. Whoever proved the stronger, he said, would have the fur cloak as a trophy and the beard of the man he had beaten. Arthur swiftly gathered his host and marched to Gwynedd.

As they approached the spears of Arthur's warriors flashed like lightning, his horses' hooves pounded the earth like thunder. For a moment Rhitta hesitated. But he was obsessed with obtaining Arthur's beard so went out to meet him on the no-man's-land between the two armies.

'As you see,' said Arthur, 'my beard is young and would not cover the gap in your mantle. But I know a beard that would serve your turn.'

'Whose is that?' asked Rhitta.

'Your own,' replied Arthur, and the laughter from his warriors echoed round the hilltops, drowning out the shouts of dismay from Rhitta's men. 'Will you fight or yield?' shouted Arthur. Rhitta's reputation as invincible king-shaver was at stake. He had no choice. He launched himself towards Arthur. Rhitta, as Arthur later admitted, was the strongest foe he'd ever met to that time. So it was a fearsome fight. But the giant king of the northern mountains, conqueror of kings, could not conquer Arthur. He had at last met his match. Arthur, though still young, was like a whirling spirit in combat, light on his feet, quick with the thrust, dodging the blade, tireless and full of surprises. Eventually Rhitta was forced to yield. It was a sad day for brute strength. And for Rhitta's own beard. Cadw of Pictland, who had shaved many a giant before, took the flaying knife and stripped Rhitta's beard in sight of both armies. Rhitta was then forced to sew his own beard into his cloak, filling the gap but with shame rather than pride.

As Arthur was leaving he turned to the defeated giant and said: 'Whose, oh king, is the firmament of Heaven?'

'Nyniaw's, for all I care,' growled Rhitta.

'And whose are the flocks and herds of stars who graze there?'

'Peibiaw's, for all I care,' Rhitta growled again.

'And who is your sovereign lord?'

'You are Arthur, and it would have been better for me if you had been long ago.'

And so Rhitta returned to his own realm much humbled in stature but wiser in knowledge. Though his beard grew muddy on the hem of his cloak it also grew into a long-lasting Welsh proverb. For it had been thick and yellow-white with black flecks like a lynx's skin. So ever after, when a man looks out on a dark winter's night and sees the snow falling thickly, he might say 'it's as thick as Rhitta's beard'!

As for Rhitta himself, it is said that when he died, Arthur's retinue carried him up to the highest peak in the mountain fastness of Eryri and built a giant cairn over his body. It was known as Gwyddfa Rhitta, Rhitta's Cairn. In time the name Rhitta was dropped and it was simply called Yr Wyddfa, The Cairn. Now, in English, it is Snowdon.

Henwen and the Monstrous Cat

Pigs were sacred to the ancient Cymru. They were regarded as a gift from the Otherworld. Their flesh was sweet and succulent, prized above all others; they were powerful beyond measure, the great wildboar Twrch Twyth being a match even for Arthur. And, as shown in this story, they could be immensely generative.

Coll, son of Collfrewy, was one of the 'Three Powerful Swineherds of the Island of Britain'. It is said that he was busy herding swine in Cornwall when one of his charges, the mighty Henwen, pregnant no less, dived into the sea. Coll had no choice but to follow, desperately clinging to her bristles. He was worried as it had been foretold that the Island of Britain would 'be the worse for her womb-burden'. They emerged dripping from the water in Gwent where, to Coll's surprise, Henwen gave birth to a litter … of wheat grains and a bee. Ever since then the fields of Gwent have been the best places for cultivating wheat and harvesting honey. A truly benign gift. Some say Henwen, meaning Old White, was in fact a Sow Goddess. She certainly had prodigious powers both to create and, as it turned out, to destroy.

From Gwent the mighty Henwen bounded to Llunion in Penfro where she bore a grain of barley and another bee. Strange piglets indeed. But, as with Gwent, henceforth this place was renowned for its barley bread and mead! Coll was somewhat relieved, but from there her next port of call was the Hill of Cyferthwch in Eryri. Here she gave birth to a wolf cub and a young eagle, and that's when the trouble started. The wolf was given to Menwaedd and the eagle to Brennach who, from that day forth, were both sorely tried by wolves and eagles, bothering their sheep and harrying their lambs.

But worse was to come. Henwen the Huge trotted briskly to Black Rock at Llanfair in Arfon and there she delivered ... a cat. Well, a kitten. But at once it was yowling and swiping with its scythe-like claws and Coll knew that this feline meant no good. So he picked it up and with all his strength hurled it into the Menai Sea. But it was a cat. That was only its first life. It swam vigorously to the shores of Môn and there was fostered by the sons of Palug. Henceforward it was known as Palug's Cat and became one of the 'Three Great Oppressions of the Island of Môn'.

This monstrous cat became quite at home in the sea and may have been the one seen chasing the boat of St Brendan, who described it thus: 'Its eyes were bigger than a brass cauldron; its teeth were like boar's tusks; furzy hair was upon him; and he had the maw of a leopard, the strength of a lion and the voraciousness of a hound.'

It is said that fair Cai, Arthur's foremost warrior (who could make himself taller than a tree, who could hold his breath for nine days and nine nights and whose body heat was so great he could keep anything dry even in the heaviest rain), went to Môn to destroy this monstrous cat. But his shield was splintered and he lost nine score of his fiercest warriors in the battle against it. After this Arthur himself assembled the army of the Island of Britain and set out to destroy Henwen, the mighty Sow Goddess, and Palug, the monstrous cat. But whether he ever did the story doesn't say.

Per edur Embarks on His Adventur e

The story of Arthur and the Quest for the Holy Grail is, perhaps, the culminating legend of British mythology. Its roots are in ancient Celtic tradition. The Grail chalice, for example, is a refinement of the Cauldrons of Rebirth and Inspiration, both found in Mabinogion tales. French poet, Chrétien de Troyes, who used oral tales he'd heard from Breton bards whose forebears had come from

Wales, wrote the story of 'Le Conte du Graal' in the late twelfth century. In it he launched the idea of the 'Quest for the Holy Grail'. His book, however, was unfinished, giving scope for other authors to develop different endings. One such author may have been the anonymous redactor of 'Peredur, son of Efrog', one of the romances in *The Mabinogion*. Although the written version of 'Peredur' post-dates Chrétien's work by 200 years, much of the material within it must have come from earlier Celtic oral sources.

In Peredur the story begins in 'the north'. It is not clear whether this means North Wales or the North of Britain, which was once Wales. Some scholars prefer this latter interpretation. However, Chrétien himself sets the beginning of the story 'high in the foothills of Mount Snowdon'. That, to me, is sufficient reason to include at least part of the tale in this collection. Of course most of it takes place in a magical 'otherworld' anyway.

There was once an earl who had seven sons. He had no interest in earning a living from his land. Rather his appetite was for tournaments, battles and war. And so, in time, he got himself killed. As did six of his seven sons. The youngest son, however, survived. His name was Peredur and while he was still young his mother, in desperation, chose to leave the realm of castles and conflict to seek refuge in the wilderness, taking with her only women, children and mild men who refused to engage in hostile pursuits. The boy was kept away from horses and weapons, and talk of heroes and jousting was expressly forbidden within his hearing.

Peredur spent long hours in the forests (near what is now Betws y Coed), playing and fashioning darts made of straight holly. He excelled at hurling these little spears with great accuracy. He was also a fast runner. He once saw two deer near his mother's herd of goats. He marvelled that they had no horns and concluded that they must be long-lost goats. So he herded them back to their enclosure. Everyone was amazed that he had the strength and speed to keep up with such fleet-footed animals.

One day three knights came riding into the forest. Their mighty steeds were decked out with all the trappings of combat; their armour glinted in the noonday sun. When the astonished Peredur asked his mother who they were she said, 'Angels'.

'Then I'll go and be an angel with them,' replied her son.

He was greeted by Owain who asked him if he'd seen a knight passing by.

'What is a knight?' asked the young innocent.

'Like me,' replied Owain.

'I will tell you if you answer my questions,' said Peredur.

'Very well,' said Owain.

'What's this?' asked Peredur, pointing to the saddle. Then he pointed to the reins, bridle, bit, stirrups, girth strap … everything, and Owain explained them all. Then Peredur said, 'Keep going and you will find what you are looking for. I will follow you as a knight at once.'

He went back to his mother. 'They're not angels, they're knights,' he said, 'and I'm going to join them.' His mother fell into a dead faint. Peredur picked out a bony nag from the horses that carried the firewood. He put a pannier on its back as a saddle. Then he twisted willow and made trappings to imitate those he'd seen on the knight's horses. He was about to leap on his nag when his mother came to. 'Wait!' she called. 'Let me give you some advice before you depart.'

'Very well,' said Peredur, 'but be quick.'

'Go to Arthur's court,' said Peredur's distraught mother. 'There you will find men generous, brave and true. If you see a church enter it and pray. If you are hungry and find food, take it, even if it is not offered. If you hear a cry of distress, especially from a woman, go to it. If you see a jewel, take it and give it to someone else. And if you see a fair maiden, be loving to her.' After giving Peredur her strange instructions his dear mother collapsed in sorrow. But Peredur was too busy to notice. He seized a fistful of his holly darts, leapt on to his wonky steed and set off after the knights.

He rode without food and drink for two days and nights through the wild forest. At last he reached a pavilion in a clearing.

Thinking it was a church he went in to pray. Inside he found a beautiful auburn-haired maiden sitting on a golden chair and wearing a golden diadem. Behind her was a table with flagons of wine, loaves of bread and a plate of pork chops. He was hungry so asked if he might eat. She said, 'Please do'. He ate half the food then spied a bejeweled ring on her finger. He explained what his mother had said and asked for the ring. She gave it to him willingly and he knelt down and kissed her. Then he mounted his horse and rode away …

Soon after the proud lord of the clearing returned. Seeing the horse's tracks he asked the maiden if anyone had been there. 'A strange-looking man,' she said. 'And was he … with you?' the knight asked. 'No, of course not,' she said. But the knight did not believe her and swore that she would not spend two nights in the same place until he had found him and avenged his imagined wrong. He set off to look for Peredur.

Meanwhile at Arthur's court another strange knight had arrived, clad in crimson armour. He swept into the hall where Arthur's retinue was and came up to Gwenhwyfar, who was holding a goblet of red wine. He seized the goblet, threw the wine over her face and breast then clouted her on the ear. 'If anyone will fight me for this goblet to avenge this insult,' he called out, 'follow me to the meadow and I will meet you there.' There was a deathly silence. Everyone assumed that this outrageous knight must be protected by magic powers, so they hung their heads, fearful of being asked to meet him.

At that moment Peredur arrived, wearing his rustic attire and riding his sorry horse with its bizarre trappings. He entered the court and asked for Arthur to make him a knight. Cai mocked him but two dwarves, who'd not spoken for a year, looked at him with wonder and said, 'God's welcome to you chief of warriors and flower of knights.' Cai cuffed and kicked them for being such idiots.

'Tall man,' said Peredur to Cai. 'Tell me, where is Arthur?'

'Be quiet you fool,' said Cai. 'Go after that knight in the meadow and take the goblet from him. Then you'll be made a knight.'

'I'll do just that,' said Peredur, and left at once.

'You shouldn't have done that,' said Owain to Cai. 'That young man is bound to be killed and that will bring disgrace on Arthur and his court.'

When Peredur found the knight in the meadow, proudly prancing back and forth, he told him that the 'tall man' had sent him to take back the goblet. 'What!' exclaimed the knight. 'Go back and tell them to send me a proper champion. I will even fight Arthur himself.'

'No, it is I who will take the goblet and your weapons,' replied Peredur. The knight, in a rage, struck the youth a mighty blow behind his head with the butt of his spear. But Peredur shot back a sharp dart at the knight. It went into the slit of his helmet, through his eye and out the back of his head, killing him stone dead.

When Owain came to investigate he was shocked to find Peredur dragging a body behind him. 'I can't get the iron tunic off him,' he said. Owain helped him remove the armour, told him to take the knight's horse and armour and return to the court to be knighted. But Peredur said, 'No, take the goblet back and tell Arthur that wherever I go I will be his man. But I will not set foot in the court again until I confront the tall man and avenge his insult to the dwarves.' And so Peredur, in proper armour and riding a fine charger, went on his way.

In the following week he met many knights, all enemies to Arthur. In each case the encounter was brief. Though Peredur was still unschooled in the arts of fighting his instincts were powerful and on every occasion his opponent was swiftly unhorsed and forced to surrender. Peredur was merciful but insisted that each one should go to Arthur and swear allegiance to him, telling the king that he was the one who sent them. 'And remind the court of my business with the tall man,' he added. This happened so many times that Arthur had to reprimand Cai, who shifted uncomfortably in his seat.

At last Peredur came to a fortress beside a lake before a forest. Two lads were fishing from a boat on the lake. A silver-haired man greeted the traveller, limped over to a blazing fire and invited him to sit down. Food was brought and after they'd eaten the aging knight tested Peredur to determine his sword-fighting skills. 'Ah,' he said. 'You will be the greatest swordsman. But let me teach you. I am your uncle, your mother's brother. You must forget what she told you and listen to me now. Be observant, but if you see something strange and no one explains it, do not ask. Only fools and spies ask questions. Let us begin.' Over the next days his uncle taught him how to manoevre his horse, and how to use a lance and sword. The youth learned at an astonishing rate and soon the old knight had taught him everything he needed.

Young Peredur continued on his way only to come to another fortress and another old uncle who again put him to the test. By means of striking an iron pillar with his sword, and breaking and repairing the sword two out of three times, the old man concluded that yes, he would be the greatest of knights but as yet he had come into only two thirds of his strength. Shortly after this a mysterious procession entered the hall with two lads carrying a bleeding lance, followed by two maidens bearing a broad platter holding a severed man's head, awash with blood. There was much wailing in the room and Peredur longed to ask what it all meant. But remembering his first uncle's counsel about questions, he said nothing …

Thus begins the story of Peredur, son of Efrog. There are countless adventures yet to go which cannot be included here. This first part of Peredur contains many parallels to 'Le Conte du Graal'. But in Chrétien's tale, where Peredur is called Percival, the lame knight became the Fisher King whose wound would not heal and whose kingdom was a wasteland. The severed head became the Grail, a bejeweled chalice emanating a brilliant light. (Incidentally some say the best candidate for the Grail Castle – if it exists in the real world – is Castell Dinas Bran, high above Llangollen on the Dee river.) When Percival, following his uncle's advice, asked no questions about the miraculous procession, the Fisher King's wound failed to heal. It would have done so – and his land would have become fertile again – if only he'd asked: 'What ails thee, uncle?' So Percival was back on his path of travails. According to another even more famous version of the story, Wolfram von Eschenbach's 'Parzival', four years later he came to a hermit in the forest (also his uncle) who told him of the Grail. In Eschenbach's story it was a 'stone from heaven':

> 'There was a war in heaven once,' said the hermit, 'where the powers of darkness ranged against the bright angels and tore the starry firmament apart. But there were those who would not take part in this war, who would not side with the darkness or the light. It was those ... neutral angels who held the universe together. Later they brought to the Earth a stone of incomparable beauty which held in its pure substance the virtues of both darkness and light. It became a stone of healing, a stone with the power to make life whole again ... Yes, there was a war in heaven once, and we my lords and ladies, lovers, contemporaries and friends; we who consist both of shadow and of light; we who are neither wholly good nor wholly bad; we sad, magpie creatures striving to be whole; we who are only human; we are the wounds of that war. So would you hear the story of the Grail, whose deep secret none may speak or tell.'

> From Lindsay Clark's 'Stone from Heaven'

The Death of Arthur

Many are the tales told of Arthur's death, many are the places where it's supposed to have happened. Perhaps not surprisingly the Welsh bards located this epic event on the mythic crown of Snowdon itself. After all there is a valley just below the summit called Cwm Llan, which could easily be anglicised into Camlann. A ridge above it is known as Bwlch y Saethau, Pass of the Arrows. A cairn of stones up there is called Carnedd Arthur, the Cairn of Arthur. Not only that, but down in the valley below is Dinas Emrys, that mysterious dragon-charged hill where Merlin first prophecied the coming of Arthur. Why would it not also be associated with Arthur's end, at least in the minds of the Welsh story makers? Despite the steep terrain of the frowning mountain perhaps these challenging peaks are a fitting backdrop for the climax to the Arthur legend.

So maybe it happened something like this.

Cwm Llan and the Pass of Arrows

Arthur was called to Dinas Emrys. He was keen to go. He hadn't been for a long time. He knew it was one of the special places of his old friend and mentor, Merlin; he knew it was a safe haven to discuss the ebb and flow of power and defeat. And his messengers had informed him that Medrawd, his own bastard son, had gathered his forces and was circling around the ancient refuge like a wasp round a jam jar. He had to be stopped. Throwing off his weariness, Arthur gathered his men and made his way to the northern mountains.

The king and 300 of his men spent the night at Dinas Emrys. Fires crackled, stories were told, songs sung. There wasn't much of a plan. In the morning they'd confront Medrawd and his host in the great valley leading up to the summit. This meant a climb over Hafod y Borth, through Cwm Llan, up to Tregalan (a town now sunk into a bog), to beneath the peak of Yr Wyddfa itself. Eagles had been seen circling high above it the day before. The omens were good, so much so that Arthur was willing to allow Medrawd the advantage of the higher ground.

It was a hard battle, uphill all the way. Medrawd's men, swooping down from the heights, had the edge over Arthur's warband, exhausted from struggling up the slope. Swords clanged, men grunted, blood flowed and mighty warriors fell. All day these two adversaries hacked and hewed at each other. But Arthur was not ready to lose a battle. With superhuman effort and aided by his invincible sword, he drove his enemy up toward the ridge until at last he was face to face with Medrawd. This would be his hardest fight. He knew he had no choice but to slay his own son. But he knew that somehow he would be slaying himself too – putting an end to the glories and ideals and valour that had been at the core of his kingdom. Better that, though, than let Medrawd ruin it all.

For a moment they faced each other off. In the stillness a raven rasped. 'I'm sorry,' said Arthur, 'I really am.' Then suddenly, with the spring of a cat, he was on him, thwacking and thrusting. He wasn't to become known as the greatest of all legendary kings for nothing. Within minutes the light had gone from Medrawd's eyes. Struggling for breath Arthur leaned on his sword and gazed out at the land stretching precipitously in all directions. Then suddenly he was down, felled by a rain of arrows loosed by the rump of his enemy. It was a cruel twist of fate. Ever after that place was known as Bwlch Saethau, the Pass of the Arrows.

In seconds Bedwyr, his most loyal companion, was by his side. 'Take me down,' wheezed Arthur, 'to the lake. The lake … a boat …' Bedwyr tried to staunch the flow of blood, then, with tears in his eyes, lifted his king and stumbled down the steep, treacherous mountainside. After a few minutes others of Arthur's surviving warband came to help and eventually the wounded king was brought to the edge of Llyn Llydaw.

Some say it was here that Arthur whispered his last command to Bedwyr to throw his sword, Excalibur, into the lake. Twice Bedwyr could not do it, fearful of what would befall Arthur and the rest of them without the protection of the invincible one. But Arthur insisted and finally Bedwyr did as he was asked. As the sword spun through the air he thought he saw a woman's arm reach out of the

water to catch it. Then out of the gloom came a black vessel moving, it seemed, without the aid of sail or oar. By now Bedwyr knew what was expected of him. The dying king was gently placed into the boat under the care of the three mysterious women who welcomed him there. Then it drifted off into the swirling mist and Arthur was gone.

The bards of old said that after the Battle of Camlann (as it became known) Arthur was taken to the Isle of Apples, Ynys Afallach. They also said that only seven of Arthur's warriors survived the battle, including Sandde Angel Face, who was so beautiful no one would spear him for fear he was an angel helping, and Morfran, son of Tegid, who was so ugly no one would spear him for fear he was a devil helping. Sadly it became known as one of the 'Three Futile Battles of the Island of Britain' because it was caused by the betrayals of Arthur's wife, Gwenhwyfar and his son, Medrawd.

Other Camlanns in North-west Wales

Recent scholars have found other locations for Camlann in north-west Wales. Steve Blake and Scott Lloyd claim, in *The Keys to Avalon*, that the Battle of Camlann took place by Afon Gamlan (the River Camlan) just north of Dolgellau in the Rhinog Mountains. There is a simple bridge over this river called Pont y Brenhin, Bridge of the King. Could this, they ask, be in remembrance of the battle?

Chris Barber and Stephen Pykitt, in their *Journey to Avalon*, claim that the Battle of Camlan took place at Porth Cadlan, to the east of Aberdaron near the end of the Llŷn Peninsula. The name, they say, translates as 'Battle Place Harbour' and near it is a rock called Maen Gwenonwy. According to Barber and Pykitt, Gwenonwy was Arthur's sister. Was the rock named after her as a result of the folk memory of the battle taking place there?

If this was the location for Camlan then nearby Ynys Enlli (Bardsey Island) could be Avalon, the mystical Isle of Apples to which Arthur was borne after receiving his fatal blow. They quote James Bonwick, from his 1894 *Irish Druids and old Irish Religions*, who said: 'The Welsh Avalon, or the Island of Apples, the everlasting source of the Elixir of Life, the home of Arthur and other mytho-logical heroes, lay beyond Cardigan Bay, the Annwn of the old sun, in the direction of Ireland.' Ynys Enlli is the only island that fits such a location. Given its traditional association with pilgrimage and the burial of saints, and given that five of the seven survivors of the Battle of Camlan were named as Welsh saints, perhaps it's not surprising that this holiest of islands could be Ynys Afallach, the 'Island of Apples which is also called Fortunate'. According to Geoffrey of Monmouth in *Vita Merlini*, Merlin and Taliesin took the wounded Arthur there and entrusted him to the care of Morgan Le Fay who, in an earlier tradition, was the daughter of Modron, widely regarded as the Mother Goddess of Celtic mythology.

Merlin, Bardsey and the Thirteen Treasures of Britain

In 1998 Andrew Clarke, a horticulturalist from the Llyn Peninsula, found a tree growing against a wall on Ynys Enlli bearing a bumper crop of apples. He took one to his friend Ian Sturrock, the apple tree man of North Wales, who swiftly ascertained that this was a unique variety of apple. It was named the 'Bardsey Apple'. The fruit was described as 'boldly striped in pink over cream, ribbed and crowned'. This new variety of apple from just one specimen tree was said to be extremely hardy and disease free. For myth and mystery lovers this was confirmation – of sorts – that this tiny island at the end of the Llyn Peninsula could well have been Ynys Afallach, the mystical Isle of Apples.

Laurence Main, author of *The Spirit Paths of Wales*, says many spirit paths and ancient pilgrim routes converge at the end of the Llyn Peninsula. Bardsey, Ynys Enlli (meaning the 'island in the current'), is a real 'Island of the Blessed', he says, where the dead were brought by boat to be laid to rest. Some 20,000 saints are said to be buried there. Considering that the island is only a mile and a half long and half a mile wide, and that nearly half of it is a steep rocky hill, that is an impressive claim. But it's an indication of how sacred the place was in antiquity. In the sixth century a Breton holy man, St Cadfan, established a monastery there. By the early Middle Ages three pilgrimages to Bardsey were deemed as beneficial to the soul as one to Rome. That's concentrated holiness!

There is a tradition that Merlin, also, ended his days on Ynys Enlli. He is supposed to have taken the 'Thirteen Treasures of Britain' with him and lived there in a 'house of glass'. The presence of such objects would seem to magnify the power of the place too. So what are the 'thirteen treasures'?

They were: the Sword of Rhydderch the Generous which, when wielded by a nobleman, burst into flames; the Hamper of Gwyddno Garanhir which, if filled with enough food for one man, when opened had enough inside for one hundred; the Horn of Brân, which would contain whatever drink the holder desired; the Chariot of Morgan the Wealthy, which could swiftly take a man wherever he wished to be; the Halter of Clydno Eiddyn which, when fixed at the foot of his bed, in the morning would hold whatever horse he wished for; the Cauldron of Dyrnwch the Giant, which would only boil a brave man's meat, never a coward's; the Whetstone of Tudwal Tudglyd which, if a brave man used it to sharpen his sword, the sword would draw blood and

kill, but for a coward it would do neither; the Coat of Padarn Red-Coat which, if a nobleman wore it would be the right size but it would never fit anyone else; the Crock of Rhygenydd the Cleric, which would contain whatever food was desired; the Chessboard of Gwenddolau, which had a board of gold and pieces of silver, and could play itself; the Mantle of Arthur in Cornwall, which would hide whoever wore it though that person could see everyone; the Mantle of Tegau Gold-Breast which, when worn by a virtuous woman was full length but when worn by a less virtuous one, was shorter; the Stone and Ring of Eluned the Fortunate which, if held in the fist, made the holder invisible.

That is quite a treasure hoard! No wonder we can't find Merlin now. He has a cloak and a ring to make himself invisible and a chariot to whisk him anywhere at will!

But what about the 'house of glass'? Some say it was a kind of solarium used for nurturing and protecting apple trees on the wind-blown island. It has even been likened to an early greenhouse. Others say that perhaps it is a metaphor for an island which is, after all, surrounded by the translucent waves of the sea, the surf its glittering walls of glass. Perhaps Ynys Enlli was itself the 'house of glass'. The idea has the ring of truth.

Or maybe we could be talking not just about the tiny island of Bardsey but the Island of Britain itself. After all, given the fragment that tells us, 'before it was taken or settled these islands were known as Clas Myrddin', Merlin's sacred enclosure, maybe long ago Merlin was the shamanic high priest of the Isles, powerful, paradoxical, all-embracing. Then the whole of Britain was indeed his 'house of glass', his 'sacred precinct'. For thousands of years. But by the end his powers and his domain had shrunk and he was compelled to take refuge with the other saints in a tiny island to the west, the 'Island of the Blessed'. He went with the treasures, his treasures, the Thirteen Treasures of Britain. Perhaps they were a concentration of his magical power and symbolised his values, the values of courage, creativity, virtue, nobility of soul, fulfillment of desire, plenty … and invisibility. Maybe it is by being in such a place as Enlli and by embodying the values of the 'Treasures' that we come close to Merlin.

The Cave of the Young Men of Snowdonia

Many are the places where a great leader is believed to lie asleep in a cave, surrounded by a ring of sleeping warriors, waiting for the time of danger when a mighty bell will ring, summoning him and his men to the rescue of the people and land. The leader has several names but in most cases it is Arthur. Not surprisingly there is one such place in Snowdonia. More surprisingly, perhaps, no mention is made of Arthur, or any other superhero. It is simply the young men of Snowdonia who lie in wait. It is known as the Cave of the Llanciau Eryri.

If, as the bards assert, Arthur was mortally wounded on the Bwlch of Arrows above and sent off in a mysterious boat to the Otherworld on Llyn Llydaw below, his warriors must have disappeared into a cave nearby. The cave is said to be on the steep cliff face of Lliwedd, sister mountain to the great Yr Wyddfa. It was found many years ago when a Cwm Dyli shepherd was looking for a sheep who had fallen over the edge of the Lliwedd precipice and was sheltering on a rock ledge far below. The shepherd, a renowned climber, lowered himself down on a rope to rescue the animal. To his astonishment he found an opening into the mountainside, hidden from below by turf and a great guardian stone. He made his way inside and found a passageway which led to a brilliantly lit cavern in the heart of the mountain. Inside he saw a numberless host of warriors, all lying asleep with white hazel wands in their hands.

Hardly breathing he watched the men for a long time, waiting to see if they would show signs of waking. But they were all soundly asleep. So he plucked up courage to explore the cave further, perhaps believing there would be treasure inside. But as he was squeezing in though the entrance his head struck a great bell, which he had not seen hanging above. A loud clanging sound echoed around the immense cavern and the warriors woke up. Springing to their feet they let out a terrifying shout. 'Is today the day?' they cried. This so frightened the shepherd that he bolted up the passage and out on to the cliff face, nearly breaking his neck as he slipped and stumbled back down to safety.

But the shepherd was never the same again. So terrified was he by this experience that he never enjoyed a day's health again. And ever since no one has dared to approach the mouth of that cave.

An old saying of the Welsh bards proves the story must be true: 'Snowdonia's youths with their white hazels will win it.'

3

THE LIVES OF SAINTS

In the fifth and sixth centuries ad there was an invasion of holy men and women throughout the Celtic lands of Brittany, Cornwall, Ireland, Scotland and Wales. Almost every other king's son was renouncing his right to rule and choosing instead to walk the path of sanctity in the name of Iesu Grist. Some of the daughters chose this way too, though their stories are often about the defence of their chastity. These pious, sometimes quarrelsome, men and women wandered the Celtic lands and seas, leaving a network of holy wells and churches in their wake. Many were located on traditional pagan sacred sites. Perhaps this continuity of reverence helps to account for the success of their mission. Many of these Christian pioneers were later canonised so the period became known as the 'Age of Saints'. Here are the stories of a few who left their names in north-west Wales.

Padarn and Peris

Llyn Padarn is one of the most beautiful lakes in Wales nestling at the foot of Snowdon. But how did it get its name? Clearly it must come from St Padarn, but neither his monastery nor any of the episodes in his relatively well-known 'Life' locate him in Snowdonia. However, in common with many other of those energetic saints, he got around. Maybe just one brief visit and blessing was enough to associate this llyn with the holy man ever after.

Padarn (or Paternicus) was born in Brittany. His 'noble parents ... availing themselves of one connection, begot Padarn'. Thereafter they dedicated themselves to the exclusive service of God and his father headed off to Ireland. When Padarn was old enough he asked his mother about his father and she said, 'He fasts, prays, watches, meditates, mourns, sleeps on a little mat and kneels to the supreme Lord day and night.' Padarn chose to follow his father's example. In the company of other monks the young man set sail for Brittania and founded a monastery at Llanbadarn Fawr near present-day Aberystwyth.

After founding this establishment he left it in the hands of a steward and dean and went to Ireland to find his father. They acknowledged each other and prayed together. At the time two Irish provinces were at war, causing much slaughter and desolation. A message, supposed to be from God, said that to bring peace both kings must see the face of a saint recently come from Britannia. The armies were summoned and Padarn was placed in their midst. 'By the grace of his countenance the devils of discord [were] driven away.'

On returning to his monastery Padarn found one of his monks whom he'd left behind in Brittany. This fellow said that he'd stood by the seashore and prayed to God saying that '[if] Padarn, whom I would follow, is indeed a saint, let the rock rise, and let it float on the waters, let the waves be made solid, let the sea harden that it drowns not the stone, [and] may I be borne in safety to the master, the leader saint Padarn'. Which he duly was. The story was met with much acclaim.

At this time Maelgwn Gwynedd was King of the North. He was on his way south to subdue troublesome tribes when he hit on an idea to trick Padarn out of his wealth. He sent messengers to the Clarach river with sacks of moss and pebbles, saying they were the contents of the royal treasury. They asked Padarn to look after it while the king went to war. Padarn agreed, but when on the king's return the sacks were found to contain only earth and stone, he was accused of theft. Maelgwn threatened to destroy the whole cloister if the treasures were not restored. In those days the veracity of a claim was tested by the accused plunging his hands into boiling water. Padarn knew he was entirely innocent and plunged his hands into the bubbling cauldron. They emerged completely unharmed. The hands of the messengers, however, were badly scalded. At that moment Maelgwn suddenly went blind. He collapsed to his knees and begged for Padarn's forgiveness. Padarn pardoned him in exchange for receiving all the land between the Clarach and Rheidol rivers. And Maelgwn's sight was restored.

Soon after David (the Welsh patron saint) received a divine message that he should take two companions, Padarn and Teilo, on a pilgrimage to Jerusalem. 'They passed together through barbarous nations receiving the gift of tongues', meaning that wherever they spoke they could address people in their own language. They were ordained as bishops by the hand of the patriarch and enriched with gifts. Padarn was given two – a splendid crozier and a richly woven tunic.

One day who should come knocking at the door of Padarn's church but 'the tyrant Arthur'! On seeing Padarn's holy tunic he said that he would like to have it for himself. 'This tunic,' said the saint, 'is not fit for anyone of a covetous nature. It is a clerical robe.' Arthur stormed out in a rage, later returning to take the tunic by force. A disciple alerted Padarn, saying that the tyrant was stamping the ground in fury. 'Then let the earth open and swallow him whole,' said the saint, and sure enough the ground opened and Arthur was buried to his chin. The humbled king then acknowledged his guilt and begged forgiveness, and the earth delivered him up. Arthur then took Padarn as a patron and went on his way. Later Padarn's tunic, or coat, became one of the Thirteen Treasures of Britain!

Saint Peris

Much less is known of St Peris, after whom Llyn Peris (the lake above Llyn Padarn), Nant Peris and Llanberis are named. He may have been one of the sons of Helig ap Glannog whose lands, by the Lavan Sands off Abergwyngregyn, were flooded in vengeance for a wicked deed. There is a legend that he was a cardinal in Rome. He may also have spent time in Bangor on Dee and later on Bardsey Island.

Near the church at Nant Peris is an ancient holy well, Ffynnon Peris. It is a square stone-lined basin with benches all around it. On the back wall there are niches to hold offerings. Peris is said to have drunk from the well daily. Adults and children came to the well to heal their rickets and rheumatism. Two trout were kept there. If they emerged during bathing the cure would be successful. If they remained hidden under the stones the visit would be in vain. This practice of keeping fish in the well is supposed to date back to the time of Peris himself. When one fish died the remaining fish lived alone in the well until it too died, then two new fish were introduced. They were expected to live up to fifty years. The last time fish were known to be added to the well was in 1896.

Cybi and Seiriol

Cybi was born in Cornwall in ad 480, son of Selif, a Cornish chieftain. He was a great-grandson of Constantine of Cornwall, who, it's thought, was also one of Arthur's forebears. Cybi's mother Gwen was not only descended from Vortigern (Gwytheyrn) but was also sister to Non, mother of St David. So Cybi had an impeccable royal and religious pedigree. Instead of succeeding his father as chieftain he chose instead to become a Christian monk.

As a young man Cybi travelled in Gaul founding churches before returning to Cornwall to do the same. He moved to South Wales, established a couple of churches in Usk, then his restless, evangelical spirit took him to Ireland. For four years he lived in a holy community on the island of Arran in Galway Bay. But after an altercation with Fintan (over one of Cybi's cows eating Fintan's vegetables) he crossed to the east of Ireland, staying briefly in Meath where he fasted for forty days and nights. But Fintan was still pursuing him so finally he and his monks crossed the Celtic Sea to the Llŷn Peninsula where he established the church and holy well at Llangybi. There he set about preaching and converting the local people.

It is said that Maelgwn, ruler of Gwynedd at the time, granted
him all the land a goat could encircle in a day. But then Maelgwn's
hounds took off after the goat, forcing it to cover a considerable distance before returning to Cybi at nightfall. Cybi did well out of the
deal. But later he fell out with Maelgwn because one of his disciples
was Caffo, brother of Gildas, who had defamed Maelgwn in his
writings. Cybi also quarreled with the locals on the Llyn who eventually threw him out. Maelgwn, reneguing somewhat, granted him
the use of an abandoned Roman fort on the western edge of Ynys
Môn where, in ad 540, Cybi founded a clâs, a monastic settlement.
This survived as a religious centre until the Reformation in the sixteenth century and was later known as Caergybi, then Holyhead.

One of the most well-known tales about St Cybi is of his friendship
with St Seiriol. Seiriol was born into a royal family based in Rhos but

chose a religious life. He lived on the north-eastern corner of Ynys Môn at Penmon, where he tended a holy well often visited by pilgrims in search of healing. Later a priory was built nearby. The two holy men loved to meet up and converse about matters of the spirit. On agreed days Cybi would set out in the morning from his monastery in the west and walk eastwards to meet his friend. The sun was on his face all morning. Seiriol, meanwhile, walked to the west in the morning with the sun behind him. After taking counsel with each other they would turn around and walk home, Cybi with the sun in his face, Seiriol with the sun behind him. In time Cybi, always facing the sun, became tanned whilst Seiriol, always with his back to the sun, remained fair-skinned. They were known, thereafter, as Seiriol Wyn, Seiriol the Fair, and Cybi Felyn, Cybi the Tanned.

It is said that Cybi was consulted on many matters of doctrine, including on the differences between the Celtic and Roman churches – long before the Synod of Whitby in ad 664. Cybi died in ad 554 at the age of 84 when 'the angels came and took his most holy soul to heaven'. Towards the end of his life Seiriol retired to Ynys Lannog where he died and was buried. Later the island was renamed by the Vikings as Priestholm but then it became known as Ynys Seiriol to honour the old saint. Since Victorian times it has been known in English as Puffin Island.

Dwynwen and Gwenfaen

In Wales the patron saint of lovers is a woman who chose never to marry and whose only experience of love was fraught with pain and sorrow. Maybe that's because in Wales, as one wag said, 'for love see tragedy'! The story goes like this.

In the mid-fifth century Brychan Brycheiniog was the ruler of the mighty kingdom of Brecknockshire. He was married three times and said to have had twenty-four daughters and eleven sons. Some of his progeny went on to have illustrious and indeed saintly careers, so much so that together they were known as one of the 'Holy Families of Britain'. The most naturally beautiful and spirited of his daughters was Dwynwen. She may have even been her father's favourite – until she fell in love with Maelon Dyfodrull, who had come down from the north. Brychan disapproved of this match – perhaps he had another suitor in mind for his special daughter – and he forbade her from seeing Maelon. But she had to see him, at least to tell him that their love could not be. The jilted lover was seized by a fit of passion and fury and tried to take Dwynwen by force. In that moment she prayed to God to cool Maelon's ardour. Little did she expect him to be turned into a block of ice, but that's what happened! Not quite what she'd meant.

Later she prayed again and asked for three things: that Maelon be pardoned for his attack, allowed to thaw out and released from his passion for her; that, as she couldn't have him, she would marry no other man her whole life long; and that instead she would devote herself to the cause of caring for lovers and soothing broken hearts … And these requests were granted.

She set off around Wales with a sister and brother, preaching and establishing churches. At last she took a boat to Ynys Môn and found a promontory cut off from the main island by the high tide. There she established a cell by a well, studied local herbal

traditions and devoted herself to healing sick animals and broken-hearted people. Her reputation spread and many came from afar to meet her, pray with her and be healed. She is thought to have died in about ad 460 after which her sanctuary became known as Llandwyn Island. It used to be believed that a sacred fish swam in the well which could predict the happiness of relationships. If a couple saw it thrashing about so energetically that the water seemed to boil, that meant love and good luck would follow them always.

Around 1500 the poet Dafydd Trefor visited the Llandwyn holy well and wrote of the miraculous healings that took place there:

Crowds on the edge of the seashore:
Girls from various regions,
An innumerable myriad of men …
Sick people, cripples and the weak bustling between holy wells,
Hill slopes covered as if with a king's army,
People from the countryside, everyone on his knees,
Wax tapers, candle wicks for health of mind,
Pipes of wine … shirts covered in stains,
A miracle as the dead are resurrected!

In modern times Dwynwen's feast day, 25 January, has become known as the Welsh Valentine's Day. And woe betide you if you live in Wales and fail to remember to treat your sweetheart that day! You might get more than the cold shoulder treatment!

Santes* Gwenfaen

Gwenfaen was born into a family of saints. Her father, Pawl Hen (Old Paulinus), was originally from the Isle of Man but is known to have founded Whitland monastery in Carmarthenshire around ad 480. He rose to become a bishop and there's a story that he was cured of blindness by Saint David himself. But Gwenfaen and her two brothers, Peulan and Gwyngeneu, lived on Ynys Môn and had cells on Holy Island.

---

*In Welsh female saints are called 'santes'.

Now Ynys Môn had also been the heartland of the Druids. Though decimated by the Romans there were some survivors who, understandably perhaps, were displeased with the influx of saints on to their island. One day they decided to take it out on Gwenfaen. They chased her away from her cell, not far from her well, near Rhoscolyn Head. But she was an agile young woman and not prepared to give herself up without a fight, or in this case, flight. She is said to have climbed a rock stack just out to sea, and when the tide came in, she was carried away by angels. That's how the site came to be known as Saints Bay.

A church in her name was founded nearby in ad 630. Her well is now one of the best preserved such chambers on Anglesey. Most of the stonework lies below ground level. There are steps that lead down to a chamber with seats in front of a pool. Traditionally the well was thought to help cure mental disorders on the payment of two white quartz stones thrown into the pool. Gwenfaen, it would seem, had cracked the secret of dealing with stress, depression, loneliness and paranoia long before these became such modern complaints.

Deiniol and Beuno

Deiniol (who gave his name to the village just over the hill from where I live) was the grandson of Pabo Post Prydain, Pabo the Pillar of Britain, who, despite his name, lost a battle with the Pictish king on the Scottish borders and was forced to relocate to Powys. Deiniol's father, Dunod Fawr, chose the pious path and was the abbot who founded the famous Bangor-is-y-Coed Monastery on the banks of the River Dee near Wrexham. This establishment was said by the Venerable Bede to be so large it was divided into seven groups each with its own superior. He also said that in ad 604 Bangor-is-y-Coed hosted a confrontation between St Augustine of Canterbury and seven British bishops.

Deiniol was said to be one of the 'seven blessed cousins' and spent his early life as a hermit on a mountain in Pembrokeshire. He is credited with several miracles whilst there. For example, when two thieves made off with his oxen in the dead of night he called after them: 'Wait, in the name of the Lord!' and made the sign of the cross. The two men were turned into standing stones. On another occasion when he could not find animals to pull his plough, out of the forest came two great stags who submitted their necks to the yoke and ploughed the ground all day long. Deiniol also went on a pilgrimage to Jerusalem and, whilst there, filled a vial of water from the River Jordan. When he returned to his Pembroke mountain he called out the name of Christ, drove his staff into the ground and poured the holy water over it. Immediately the staff grew into a beautiful tree and a fountain of the sweetest water sprang up from the spot. That water had healing powers and many people came from as far as Oxford to be cured of serious ailments.

At the time there was a church at Bangor on the Menai Strait. When the prior of that place died the heavens directed that messengers should be sent to find a hermit in Pembroke whose name was Deiniol (Daniel). He would be the new pastor of the church. Despite his illustrious forebears Deiniol considered himself to be lacking in formal education. So he was astonished when messengers came looking for him and said humbly that he 'was no prophet'. But he was persuaded by their insistence and followed them back to Bangor. As he entered the city the bells began to ring of their own accord. Deiniol was led to the high altar and when he rose from his prayers he was 'fully endowed with ecclesiastical knowledge'.

Maelgwn Gwynedd favoured the monastery with land and privileges, later raising it to the rank of a bishopric. Deiniol was the first bishop and lived there the remainder of his days. In ad 545 he attended the Synod of Llandewi Brefi with St David when the subject of rules for penance were being discussed. He died in ad 584 and was buried on Bardsey Island.

Saint Beuno

On the pilgrimage route to Bardsey at the beginning of the Llŷn Peninsula is the very fine church of Clynnog Fawr. It is dedicated to St Beuno and this is his story.

Beuno was another son of a royal household who eschewed political power and chose instead to become a man of the cloth. He was born in Powys around ad 545 and educated in the monastery at Bangor-is-y-Coed, also known as Bangor on Dee. When his father died he planted an acorn, which grew into a mighty oak. One branch curved down to the ground and rose again making a great arch. Later it was said that 'if an Englishman should pass between this branch and the trunk of the tree, he would immediately die; but should a Welshman go, he would in no way suffer'.

Next Beuno was granted land at Berriew, near Welshpool, in Montgomeryshire. A standing stone, 'Maen Beuno', marks the spot where he is said to have preached. One day, when he was walking by the Severn, he heard the cries of a Saxon hunting across the river and said to his disciples, 'My sons, put on your clothes and let us leave now. For the nation of that man with the strange language … will invade this place … and they will hold it as their possession.'

After this Beuno headed north and built a place of worship at Treffynon, now known as Holywell. There he daily instructed his niece, a girl called Gwenfrewy (Winifred), in the ways of the Christian Church. But she had a suitor, Caradoc, who was not pleased when she decided to become a nun. The story goes that he cut off her head which rolled downhill and where it stopped a healing spring appeared. Beuno, however, miraculously joined her head back to her body and her life was restored. Seeing the murderer leaning on his sword with a defiant air, Beuno invoked God's wrath and Caradoc dropped dead on the spot and was swallowed up by the ground.

Some time later Beuno headed west to Arfon near the mouth of the Seiont river. There he was offered the township of Clynnog 'without tribute or service, or anyone having any claim on it'. Beuno readily accepted and, from then onwards, Clynnog was his main abode. He built an abbey there and died in ad 640. He was buried in the chapel on the south-west side of the church.

There is a story told of St Beuno at Clynnog that often on a Sunday he would walk north across the waters of Caernarfon Bay to preach at Llandwyn Island, home to St Dwynwen. He always carried his book of sermons under his arm. One day when he was returning he dropped his precious writings into the water and failed to recover them. This concerned him greatly as much work goes into the writing of sermons. However, when he reached dry land he was relieved to find the book on a stone out of reach of the tide with a curlew mounting guard over it. The holy bird had picked it up and brought it to safety. Thereupon St Beuno knelt down to give thanks and to pray that the curlew be always protected by the Creator. And so it has been ever since. To this day it is very hard to find where that elegant, long-beaked bird lays its eggs.

4

THE TYLWYTH TEG

Tylwyth Teg – usually translated as 'Fair Folk' though strictly meaning 'fair tribe' – is the main name for fairies in Wales. Belief in them persisted long after the coming of Christianity. Even now, in the magical glades of Eryri, the Llŷn and Môn, it's not hard to imagine them. They live in lakes and hollow hills and, at special times of the year, emerge to play enchanting music, dance in rings and ride on fairy ponies. They are afraid of iron, which suggests they may derive from a memory of earlier Neolithic peoples. They can bestow riches on those they favour but can also wickedly kidnap fair-haired children, replacing them with withered 'change-lings'. Occasionally fairy maidens marry human men but they always wish to return to their own. Time with the Tylwyth Teg passes slowly, so an hour in fairy time is a year in ours! The story of 'Fairy Ointment' in this chapter is found elsewhere in Britain but is firmly believed to have also happened here! I've also included a well-known story about witches in this section.

The Fairy Wife

It's not so easy to see them now. But there was a time when, on windless moonlit summer nights near Betws Garmon by Llyn Cwellyn on the flanks of Snowdon, if a man was to go out into a certain field and hide behind a certain hedge and keep himself quite still, and if he were patient long enough, he might, if he was lucky, see the Fair Folk dancing and hear their soft, sweet music play. Evan, from Ystrad Farm, knew this. And so, when such a rare night came round, he would slip out, creep up, kneel down and watch the Fair Folk play. He was utterly enchanted.

On one of those magical nights he decided he had to get closer. So he crawled silently through the grass toward the fairy ring until he could almost reach out, grasp a hand and be swept into the dance. The fairies were captivating, swirling around, tossing their heads, stamping their feet, swinging each other around. Evan watched, his eyes growing wider, his mouth drier. One of the fairies caught his eye more than the others. She was more beautiful than any human he'd ever seen. Her hair was pale primrose gold, her skin was like cream, her cheeks flushed like the wild rose. As she swept past him he could hear her singing as sweetly as a nightingale. She danced with such elegance and grace Evan knew he would not be happy until he could make her his wife.

When the merrymaking was at its height, without quite knowing what he was doing, he sprang up, ran forward and snatched up the maiden in his arms. Then he turned and hurtled home, the fairy damsel struggling under his grip, the other fairies shouting behind them. He did not stop until he reached his house and locked the door behind him. The iron bolt meant it was impossible for the Fair Folk to reclaim her for they are terrified of touching iron.

He placed the fairy maiden in a soft chair and knelt before her. 'I'm sorry to take you from your people. I know it must be upsetting. But I love you and I really want you to be my wife. Please.' But the maiden, looking at him with her large, sky-blue eyes just shook her head. 'I will do anything to win your love,' said Evan. 'I am kind and helpful. You will grow to love me in time.'

When she spoke at last her voice seemed to fill the room with honey and birdsong. 'No,' she said. 'I cannot love a human and I want to return to my people. I won't stay here. Please, please let me go.' But Evan would not give in. He begged and pleaded with her, and when she realised he wasn't going to change his mind she said, 'Alright, I will stay with you for now but I cannot be your wife. If you can guess my name I will be your maidservant.'

Evan was disappointed, but thought in time he could persuade her to marry him. 'Do you fairies have special fairy names,' he asked, 'or names like other Welsh girls?'

'Find out,' she said.

'Catrin, Siwan, Angharad, Bethan?' he asked.

'No, no, no, no,' she said.

That evening he kept guessing using all the Welsh names he could think of: 'Blodwen, Mari, Eluned, Sian ... Elen, Olwen, Gwyneth, Mai ... Rhiannon, Branwen, Myfanwy?' She kept shaking her head. In the morning he carried on, trying all the English names he knew: 'Janet, Judith, Sally, Lynn?' He even made up what he thought might be fairy names: 'Celery, Bluebell, Stardust, Sparkle.' But no, no, no, no. He began thinking he would never guess and became despondent. However, he wasn't willing to give up.

That day Evan had to go to Caernarfon market. On the way home he spied a group of Fair Folk talking animatedly by a pond behind some trees. They seemed to be in a council, and he wondered if they were talking about how to get their sister back. He inched closer until he could hear their voices. They were indeed discussing the fate of the girl he'd kidnapped. 'Oh it's a terrible thing she's been taken,' said one. 'Yes, dreadful,' said another. 'Penelope, Penelope,' cried out a third. 'Why did you go away with a mortal man?'

'Aha! Penelope,' Evan murmured to himself. 'So that is the name of my sweetheart!' And he crept away without making a sound.

Back home he slipped in through the door and found his fairy sitting on the floor. He sat down beside her and said, 'Penelope my heart of gold. You are the one for me.'

Tears sprang to her eyes and for several minutes she wept. As her sobs subsided she asked, 'But who told you? Who revealed my name?' Evan explained how he had heard her sisters talking. Then Penelope sighed deeply, wiped her eyes and said, 'Alright then, I will keep my bargain. I will be your maid.'

And so it was that Evan's life improved radically. Everything Penelope did she did to perfection. She kept the house clean, bought food economically and ran the farm well. Whether they, too, were under her spell who knows, but the cows produced creamier milk, the hens laid larger eggs, the sheep sported finer fleeces and the cabbages grew twice as round. The butter she churned was prized in the marketplace, the blankets she knitted always sold first. Evan was happy, of course, but he still longed to make her his wife and to take her to his bed. He did not give up asking, knowing as he did the old Welsh proverb: 'Many a blow makes the stone break.' And at last she did give in. Maybe by now she'd grown truly fond of him. But there was a condition she wanted to impose which harked back, perhaps, to the origin of the Tylwyth Teg in the early peoples who worked this land before the coming of metals …

'I will marry you,' she said. 'But if you ever strike me with iron our marriage will be over and I will return to my Fair Folk family.' Evan thought this a little strange but knew he would never strike her with anything and readily agreed. He was delighted that at last they could be husband and wife. And so they were, and lived happily together. Soon enough a son was born, followed by a daughter, and they were the images of their mother and the idols of their father. So wise and active was the fairy wife that Evan became one of the most prosperous farmers in the area, farming all the land to the summit of Snowdon.

One summer's day Evan went out to a field near the house to catch a filly. He was planning to sell her at the Caernarfon Fair. But she was a high-spirited creature and would not be easily bridled. So he called out to Penelope for help. She came and together they drove the frisky young horse into the corner of the field. Evan was approaching her with the bridle when again she broke loose. He'd lost his patience by now and in a fit of fury hurled the bridle after her. But it missed its mark, flew past the filly, striking his wife on the cheek with the iron bit. And in that instant Penelope disappeared. One moment she was standing there, laughing to see her husband so cross. The next moment she was gone. Though it had been an accident, Evan had broken his word and no matter how far and wide he searched, he never saw his beloved fairy wife again.

However … it is said … she could not forget her love for her children and husband. Though the law of her people forbade her from walking the earth again after her return to the Tylwyth Teg, she made a small grassy island which floated on Cwellyn Lake. And from there she was able to spend many an hour happily conversing with her husband and children on the shore. And the floating island, they say, can still be seen to this day.*

Penelope's children and their descendants were known as Pellings, a name deriving from the original Penelope.

The Fairy Harp

A company of fairies who lived in the recesses of Cader Idris were in the habit of going about the countryside in disguise, testing the dispositions of the cottagers. Those who gave them a welcome received favours. Those who did not had bad luck for the rest of their days.

Old Morgan ap Rhys was sitting one night by himself in his own chimney corner, enjoying his pipe and his pot of Llangollen ale. The generous liquor made him feel lighthearted, so when there was a gentle rap at the door he called out amiably, 'Come in, come in, whoever you are.' The door opened and in came three travellers, actually fairies in disguise. Perhaps Morgan had an inkling of who they were, for when one asked if they might have a little food as they were poor and hungry, he replied, 'Of course, help yourself. As long as my name is Morgan I'll never refuse anyone in need.'

Kindness begets kindness, and as the 'travellers' were putting some bread and cheese into their pouches they informed him that they could grant him any wish he liked. Now Morgan, who was fond of music, had no difficulty in deciding: 'Well it is the wish of my heart,' he said, 'to have a harp that will play a lively tune under my fingers, no matter how ill I strike it.' No sooner was his request made than a splendid harp appeared before him. And his guests … vanished.

---

*This floating island seems to have been referred to by Giraldus Cambrensis in his 1191 *Journey Through Wales* in which he wrote: 'At the top of these mountains [is a remarkable] … lake … [It] has a floating island which moves about and is often driven to the opposite side by the force of the winds. Shepherds are amazed to see flocks that are feeding there carried off to distant parts …'

This, of course, was no ordinary harp. It was a fairy harp and it did indeed play sprightly tunes despite the player's lack of art. Soon his wife came in bringing some friends. Morgan was keen to show off his new gift and his skill upon it. When he began to play, the music pouring forth from the enchanted strings was so infectious and exhilarating that the whole company sprang to their feet and danced around the room. In their wild abandon they knocked over chairs, bumped into tables, jolted each another and jumped so high they cracked their heads on the ceiling. Soon they realised there was something uncanny about the harp and called on Morgan to stop. But he was enjoying the laughter and capers he was inducing in his friends and ignored their appeals. Until at last he himself was so exhausted he finally put the magical instrument down.

The news that Morgan had come into possession of a harp with mysterious powers was hot gossip around the district and many visitors came to see him. Whenever he played everyone was irresistibly impelled to dance and could not leave off until he stopped. Even lame people and once a one-legged man found themselves cavorting about.

But after a while Morgan's fairy harp became a problem, for his playing did much damage to the good folks in the neighbourhood. Limbs got dislocated, furniture was smashed. For whoever heard the sound could not help themselves. They *had* to dance. It might have been fun to start with, but it always got out of hand. Finally, after a very vigorous performance one night, the next morning Morgan could not find his harp anywhere. It had disappeared as suddenly as it had arrived. Had his neighbours taken it? Or perhaps it was the fairies feeling sorry for the poor dancers. Whichever it was Morgan never was able to display his musical prowess again.

THE Girl and the Golden Chair

Long ago on the slopes of Moel y Ci – above where Rhiwlas is today – the early peoples worked the land and built thatched roundhouses on platforms cut from the steep ground. The ruins of their homes can still be found on the hillside today, buried beneath bracken and bramble. A couple of thousand years later another family was to be found in a farmstead on that hill, working hard as their ancestors had done. The soil was thin and the winds were strong, but it was good country for sheep. They grew a few vegetables and kept a pig, but sheep were the mainstay of the farm.

The farmer and his wife had a daughter called Mari. Mari was a cheerful soul with a winning smile and a willing hand. Whatever she did she did well and one of those things was knitting. When the wool from the sheep's back was carded and spun there was always the knitting to do. Socks and jumpers were much needed and sold well in the Caernarfon market. So Mari became a good knitter. But she often had to go on to the mountain to look after the sheep, especially in the lambing season. So she developed the art of knitting whilst walking, a very handy thing to do. A ball of wool in her bag, a pair of knitting needles in her hands and she'd be back after a day with a new stocking under her arm.

The fairies liked Mari, approving of her goodness and industry, and wanted to give her a reward. One day when she was walking up a steep sheep track high on the hill she looked up from her knitting and she saw ahead of her, by the bank of a trickling stream, something golden, shining brightly in the midday sun. She ran to it and found to her amazement that it was a chair. She ran her fingers over it. It was real alright and absolutely beautiful. She sat down. It fitted her perfectly and was so comfortable.

Mari was about to fall into a reverie when she remembered that when fairies give you a gift you have to take it at once or it will disappear. So she tried to lift the chair ... but it was too heavy for her. Hmmm. The fairies hadn't thought of that. Here she was on the wild mountainside with no one to help her. If she went home now to get help she might never find her way back. Then she looked at her knitting and ball of wool. She had an idea. She swiftly tied one end of the yarn to the chair and began walking down the hill, unrolling the wool as she went. She'd be able to follow the thread back to the chair. But before she could see the farmhouse the wool ran out. Then she remembered the stocking. She'd have to sacrifice her morning's work. She pulled out a thread from her stocking, tied it on and continued walking, unraveling as she went. When she came to the end of that she was within sight of home.

Mari called out to her mother and father but they didn't hear her. So she put a stone on the end of the wool and ran down to the farm. She poured out her story about the golden chair to her parents and urged them to help. They ran back up the hill together but no yarn under a stone could they find. All afternoon they searched but found not a whisper of wool nor a glimmer of the golden chair. At last they were driven home by the coming dusk. The following day they renewed their search covering every inch of ground but with no success. The fairies must have removed both the golden chair and the thread that led to it. If only the yarn had been long enough the golden chair would have been Mari's forever.

Some say the golden chair is still somewhere hidden away on that mountain. But it's no use looking for it. It will only be revealed by chance to the one fated to find it.

Fair y Ointment

Tomos and Beth, the old couple who lived at Garth Dorwen Farm near Penygroes, were in need of a maidservant. So they went to All Hallows Fair in Caernarfon to the place where the young men and women who were looking for work would stand. There they saw a beautiful girl with red hair and green eyes, standing apart from the others. They asked if she wanted a place and if she could spin and sew, clean and cook. And as she did and she could they said 'good' and away she went with them. Her name was Eilian.

At that time it was customary during the winter months for the womenfolk to spin after supper. Eilian was happy to do it, but on nights when the moon grew full she would take her wheel out to the field and spin in the moonlight. She said she could see better out there. On one such night Beth was peering through the window looking down to Eilian's field when she saw the Fair Folk dancing in circles around Eilian and skeins of fine-spun wool piling high. She shook old Tomos awake and they were both astonished at the wondrous sight they saw. In the morning, sure enough, Eilian presented them with a copious quantity of finely spun yarn, much to the satisfaction of the old couple. This continued all winter long.

Spring advanced and the days grew bright. Then one morning, towards the end of April, when Eilian had been spinning outside again, there was no sign of her. She had disappeared and everyone said she had gone with the fairies. And that was that.

Now old Beth was known in those parts as the best of midwives. Many months after Eilian's disappearance on another moonlit night there was a clatter of hooves on the cobblestones outside their house. Tomos went to the door with a poker. He wasn't expecting anyone at this hour. It was a gentleman in black who'd come for the services of the midwife. His wife, he said, was in labour. Naturally Beth gathered her bag together, pulled on her cloak, and, with a little help, climbed on to the back of the horse.

She rode behind the stranger through a fine mist along narrow tracks up the valley till they came to Rhos y Cowrt. In the mouth of a cave they dismounted and went inside. There on a bed of straw at the back of the cave with a few tapers lit around her was a woman, already in the throes of labour. In the dim light old Beth did her midwifery business and soon the child was born. It was

only when she was putting the newborn babe to its mother's breast that she realised with a shock that the woman was none other than her former maidservant Eilian.

Soon after the husband came in and handed the midwife a little jar of ointment. 'Put a smear on each of the child's eyelids,' he said. 'But be sure not to put it on your own eyes,' he added, 'or it will be the worse for you!'

'Oh no,' replied Beth. 'Why should I ever do that?' She unscrewed the lid and rubbed a little of the blue ointment on to each of the baby's eyelids. Then she busied herself about the place cleaning things up. Suddenly her left eye began to itch. Without thinking what she was doing she rubbed it with her finger – which still had some ointment on it. And when she opened that eye she saw another world.

Eilian was lying on a four-poster bed, there were chandeliers hanging from the ceiling, tapestries on the walls and fairy folk running hither and thither bringing titbits for the mother to eat. It was the most beautiful place she'd ever seen. But with her right eye she still saw the dim, dank cave.

When at last they were left alone old Beth went up to Eilian: 'Hello my dear,' she said. 'I see you now have many friends in this marvellous place.'

'Er … yes,' replied Eilian. 'But how do you know?'

'Oh, I accidentally rubbed my eye with the ointment,' explained Beth.

'Be sure my husband doesn't find out,' said Eilian, then she told Beth what had happened. 'The fairies helped me with the spinning,' she said, 'as long as I agreed to marry one of them. But I always took a knife out with me to guard against being kidnapped. And at night in bed I covered myself with a rowan branch, as the fairies will not cross wood from that tree. But on the evening after we sheared the sheep I was so tired I grew careless and forgot the branch. That was when they snatched me away. And by the way,' she added, 'what you see with your right eye is the reality of things. With the left eye you see only the illusion of fairy glamour.'

Beth kept her secret from Eilian's husband and the next day was paid handsomely and taken home. Some time later she went again to the market in Caernarfon. She arrived late and a friend said that the fairies must be there because the noise was growing and the prices rising. Then, with her left eye, the old woman spied the fairies and saw Eilian's husband standing by a stall nearby, putting apples into a bag. Without thinking she went up to him and said, 'Good day sir. How are Eilian and the baby?'

'They are well,' he replied cautiously, 'but with which eye do you see me?' Again without thinking Beth pointed to her left. In a flash the fairy picked up a bulrush and plucked out her eye. Aieeee!

From that day on Beth never saw the fairies again. Her one good eye had to do the work of two for the rest of her life.

And still now there is a field at Garth Dorwen called Cae Eilian where the red-haired, green-eyed girl did her spinning. Which proves the story must be true!

The Changeling

This story comes from Capel Curig in the heart of the mountains of Eryri.

A farmer's wife had given birth to a bonny baby at the beginning of the harvest, but as the weather was poor and the farm was a long way from her church, she neglected to baptise it before the usual eighth day. In the midst of this unsettled weather came one fine day. Determined to do what she could to save the harvest she went to the field, leaving the baby in the charge of its grandmother who was, by now, rather frail and forgetful and who promptly fell asleep.

This was the fairies' chance and they took it. The creature in the cradle soon began to whine and groan and make a terrible racket, waking the old woman. When she looked at it she was horrified to see that the fretful child was skinny and wizened and was moving restlessly about in its crib. 'Oh dear,' she murmured to herself, 'the Old Tylwyth have been here.' At once she blew the horn and the mother came running home.

She went straight to the cradle, lifted the child out, hugged him, sang to him, tried in everyway to soothe him. But it was to no avail. He continued to scream. Finally she had a good look at him and realised to her dismay that this wasn't her child at all. The more she looked at him the uglier he became. So she sent for her husband and asked him to call for a *gwr cyfarwydd*, a skilled man. Someone told him that the parson of Trawsfynedd was skilled in dealing with such things, so he travelled through the mountains to find him.

The parson directed him to take a shovel, to cover it with salt and to cut a cross in the salt. Then he should take it into the room where the changeling was and, after opening the window, put it on the fire until the salt was burnt. This they did and when the salt got white-hot the 'peevish abortion' screamed one last time and vanished into thin air. And on the doorstep, to their great relief, they found their own child, whole and unscathed.

Lost Cow and Daughter

Evan Gruffydd of Anglesey had two fine possessions that made him a happy man. One was his lovely daughter, Olwen, the apple of his eye. She was as quick as a sparrow, bright as moonshine and laughed the whole day long. The other was his wonderful dappled brown cow who yielded buckets of rich, creamy milk.

One morning when Olwen went to the byre to milk the cow, she found the cow was gone. Their prize animal had disappeared. Troubled by their loss, Evan and Olwen set out at once to find her. Down lanes, across fields, through hedges, over ditches they went, asking everyone if they'd seen the dappled brown cow.

But nobody had. All the cows they saw belonged to other people. And nowhere did they see such a fine cow as theirs. They spent the whole day on this fruitless search.

Coming home in the evening, Evan spotted in the distance something strange. As they went closer he realised it was a band of fairies galloping round in a ring on their little ponies. Olwen was curious. It was the first time she'd seen such a thing. They crept forward through the long grass until Evan said, 'Stop now, we're near enough. Any closer will be dangerous.'

But Olwen was irresistibly drawn onward. Before her father could stop her she was on the edge of the Tylwyth Teg circle. And then … she was in. Immediately she disappeared from view along with the tiny frisking ponies and their fearless fairy riders.

Evan Gruffydd forgot about his lost cow. His lost daughter was much more important to him. Frantically he searched the fields but in vain and eventually, as the dark descended, he was forced home. To his surprise and relief he found that the dappled brown cow had returned of her own accord. That was something, at least. But in the days that followed his quest for his beloved Olwen drew a blank.

Finally he went to see an old friend of his who was wise in the ways of the fairy world and he came up with a plan. 'Unfortunately,' he said, 'you will have to be patient and wait a whole year. Then, on the anniversary of her disappearance, go back to the exact same spot at the exact same hour. Take with you four of your strongest friends.' The wise man then explained what he should do.

The year passed slowly for Evan Gruffydd. Though his cow continued to give plenty of milk he could not be happy without Olwen. At last the day came for the plan to be put into effect. He and his four trusty, strapping friends went down to the fields and hid in the long grass. Then they heard the sound of tiny hooves and saw the fairies galloping around in a ring. And there, in their midst, was Olwen, riding round on a pony of her own.

Evan tied a sturdy rope around his waist and gave the end to his friends to hold. Then he crept up to the fairy circle, quickly dashed in and grabbed hold of his daughter. With his arms firmly around her, he gave a signal to the men who began pulling on the rope. Though the magic of the fairy ring was strong the men were stronger and they managed to drag Olwen and her father out of it to safety.

'Oh cariad,' said Evan with tears in his eyes. 'So good to have you back again.'

Olwen looked dazed and puzzled. 'What do mean father?' she said. 'I've only been gone a minute. Come on, let's go home and we'll look for the cow again tomorrow.'

'We found the cow a year ago,' said Evan with a smile. 'And that's how long you've been gone!'

Olwen was bemused. 'In that case,' she said, 'it is very good to be back.' And she gave him a big kiss on the cheek and ran laughing all the way home.

The Witches of Llanddona

Ynys Môn is at the heart of the Celtic Sea so from time to time those who'd been lost at sea or cast adrift elsewhere found themselves washed up on its rugged or, if they were lucky, sandy shore. Early in the sixteenth century one such group of men and women were beached in a small boat at Red Wharf Bay near the village of Llanddona. People are often wary of strangers and the locals in that area were no exception. Thinking they might be miscreants pushed rudderless out to sea to meet their fate, they tried to drive them away. But two men from the half-starved, thirsty crew forced themselves ashore and, striking the ground with a staff, made a spring of pure water burst forth. This miracle impressed, or perhaps terrified, the locals and the newcomers were allowed to stay. And for ever after they were associated with the village. For it transpired they were a family of witches and they became known as the infamous Witches of Llanddona.

The men, it was said, lived by smuggling but if anyone should try to arrest them they fought like lions. Then, when their strength began to fail, they'd open the knot of their neckerchief and release a fearsome black fly, which flew into the eyes of their opponents, disorienting them. The women, with dishevelled hair and bared breasts, visited farmhouses and requested charity, more as a right than a favour, and no one dared refuse them. They paid for nothing at the markets and no stallholder was brave enough to insist that they did.

There was one, however, who did stand up to the witches. His name was Goronwy ap Tudor and he was canny in dealing with witchy ways. He knew how to break their spells. A birthmark on his chest made him believe he was protected. He nailed horseshoes above every door, laid rings of rowan beneath the doorposts, sprinkled soil from the churchyard around his house and in the animal byres too. He kept a supply of dried adder skins which he ground into a powder to sprinkle on bewitched cows, pigs and sheep. His chief adversary was Bella Fawr. She took to working magic against Goronwy's cattle. One day when he went to fetch them from the meadow to be milked he found them sitting like cats before a fire, their hind legs beneath them. Goronwy took the adder skin powder and scattered it over their horns. They got up at once and walked with their usual dignity into the byre.

One moonlit night Goronwy was walking home past the field where he kept his three best cows. He noticed a large hare hanging on to the teat of one of them, which was trying to shake it off. It sucked the teat, spat out the milk then went to the next teat and did the same. It was trying to suck his cows dry. He knew that this hare was Bella Fawr so the next night he loaded his shotgun with silver coins (as shot cannot penetrate a witch's body) and placed vervain under the stock for good measure. When he saw the hare milking the cows he fired, hitting it in the legs. The hare ran off in the direction of Bella's cottage, with Goronwy after her. When he reached her house he heard dreadful groans. Through the window he could see no hare, but old Bella by the fire with blood streaming from her legs. After that he was never troubled by her in the shape of a hare again.

However, she did not give up on her feud with him. She was determined to have her revenge. When she had recovered from her injuries she went to Ffynnon Oer, the cold cursing well, and launched at him the great curse of the Witches of Llanddona:

> May he wander for ages many,
> And at every step, a stile,
> At every stile, a fall;
> At every fall, a broken bone,
> Not the largest nor the least bone,
> But the chief neckbone, every time.

The curse worked. Goronwy's bones ached and seemed to be crumbling away within him. He had no strength. He knew he must act fast. He went to a great oak tree near his farm and scraped off a fungus called witch's butter. He squeezed it into a shape, went to Bella's cottage, called out her name and began sticking pins in the butter. Straight away screams of pain issued forth from the cottage. Then the door swung open and it was Bella begging him to stop. 'I will only stop,' panted Goronwy, 'when you say: "God's blessing on you, Goronwy Tudor, and all you possess".'

'No!' cried out Bella.

With the last of his strength Goronwy stuck another pin in. At last, between screams of agony, she wheezed out the blessing. Goronwy felt his strength return and slowly removed the pins.

After that neither Bella, nor any of her tribe, had any power over Goronwy, his wife, animals or possessions, ever again.

5

FOLK TALES

Folk tales are usually about archetypal or generically named characters and have a meaning that expresses key aspects of a culture. Often there are several versions of the tale. Some of those that follow – such as 'The Faithful Hound' and 'The King with Horse's Ears' – may have come from afar but they have put down strong roots in the rocky soil of Snowdonia. 'The Eagle and the Wren' was known to Aristotle. The stories of 'The Harpist and the Key' and 'A Wedding in the Dark' were told by my Taid (my Welsh grandfather) and were passed on to me by my parents.

Cadwalader's Goat

Once there was a goatherd called Cadwalader who grazed his shaggy, long-horned beasts on the flanks of the great Yr Wyddfa. He was especially fond of a she-goat he called Jenny. On weekends he combed her hair free of tangles and talked to her as if she were human.

But one warm summer evening she turned away from his friendship and skipped off up the mountain. Instantly Cadwalader gave chase, calling her name, pleading with her to come back. It was hard work running up the hill. The slopes were steep, the paths were rough and soon he was breathless. Sometimes she'd stop and wait until he'd almost caught up, then off she'd go again. With soaked feet and bruised knees he was furious with her for leading him on this merry dance. But his shouts and threats made not the slightest difference.

At last she came to a crag with a steep chasm below it. Over the gap was another crag and the high mountain beyond. And there was Jenny coolly looking at him as if to say, 'Come and get me!' Utterly exasperated, Cadwalader picked up a heavy rock and as she sprang across the chasm he let fly. He hit her in the side and she fell whimpering to the rocks beneath. Cadwalader was devastated. He carefully picked his way down to where she lay and knelt beside her. She was still alive but only just. As he stroked her head she licked his hand. 'Oh Jenny,' he cried. 'What have I done? Can you ever forgive me?'

Cadwalader sat with her head on his lap, caressing her hair and speaking gently to her. As the dusk settled she grew quieter and calmer. Then a shaft of moonlight pierced the clouds and when Cadwalader looked down he was startled to see that Jenny was no longer a goat.

She had turned into a beautiful young woman with silky hair and soft brown eyes. Not only that, instead of being at death's door she was smiling and looking very pleased with herself. She sat up and, taking hold of his hand, said, 'Cadwalader I have found you at last!'

Cadwalader's heart pounded. He wasn't sure he wanted to be found in this way. She was a lovely lass sure enough, but wasn't she also a goat? He felt very mixed up. But he couldn't dwell on emotions long for Jenny sprang to her feet, took his hand in hers and set off nimbly up the mountainside. He had no choice but to follow. Her hand was soft and firm like a woman's, but once in a while he was sure he could feel a hoof. And though her laughing conversation was lively and tender, he was sure that now and again he could hear her bleat. He was in a bad place, he knew it, but felt it could only get worse.

High on the mountain they came to a wide, level rocky shelf. It was thronging with goats of many colours sporting shaggy beards and long curving horns. Kids leapt about everywhere. There was a chorus of bleating the like of which Cadwalader had never heard. Jenny, the now-woman, thrust her way through them until at last she came to the greatest billy-goat of them all. There she stopped and drew Cadwalader to her side. She spoke to the goat as if to a king. 'Oh King Billy,' she said. 'This is him.'

'Hmm,' grunted the king. 'I'd expected something better. He looks a feeble sort to me.'

'He'll be better after,' said Jenny hopefully.

'After what?' wondered Cadwalader.

The king grunted again then turned his black eyes to Cadwalader and said, 'Do you take this Jenny to be your lawful, wedded nanny?'

'Ah!' exclaimed Cadwalader to himself, 'they want to turn me into a goat!' 'No!' he cried out. 'I don't want to be a goat. I don't want to have anything to do with goats!'

'Don't want to be a goat!' roared King Billy. 'But we are the lords of creation. In that case we'll have nothing more to do with you!' And with that he lowered his mighty horns and charged at Cadwalader, knocking him clean off the side of the mountain.

And poor Cadwalader tumbled and rolled down and down and didn't stop till he reached the bottom.

In the morning he woke up with his head in a bush, his feet in a bog and black and blue all over. But the sun was shining and the birds were singing so he picked himself up, brushed himself off and hobbled all the way home. After that he never saw Jenny – goat or girl – again. In fact he gave up on goats altogether. He sold his herd and bought sheep instead.

That's why today the farmers of Eryri all keep sheep. But if you're lucky you might just catch a glimpse of a wild goat, magnificent and brooding. Just don't get close enough to stroke its hair!

The Afanc

The lands of the Conwy Valley were flooding – again. But it was not due to endless rain. The farmers knew it was because the Afanc, a monstrous beast living in Llyn-yr-Afanc in the River Conwy, had been stirring. And whenever he thrashed about in his pool the waters broke over its bank and flooded the regions below. Crops were ruined, livestock drowned. Attempts to kill him failed because his hide was so tough that no spear or arrow could pierce it.

At last a meeting was held in the Llanrwst market square. 'Something must be done,' the farmers declared. 'We have lost too many sheep in the floods caused by this troublesome brute.'

'If we cannot kill him perhaps we can drag him out of the lake and take him somewhere he won't make so much trouble. One of the lakes higher up Snowdon perhaps.' 'But how can we hold him? How can we move him?' There seemed no answer to such questions.

Then a blacksmith spoke up and said, 'I will make strong iron chains to hold him.'

And a drover said, 'Let us ask Hu Gadarn if we can use his two mighty oxen to move the Afanc. They are the twin calves of the Freckled Cow and the strongest beasts of all.'

So it was agreed. The iron chains were forged and the long-horned oxen of Hu Gadarn were brought. One problem remained.

Most days the Afanc lurked in the murky depths of its lake. How would they coax him out? The answer came from a brave and beautiful farmer's daughter called Siân. 'They say that the Afanc likes young women,' she said. 'I will sing him out of the water.'

And sure enough that's what she did. Siân went to the Afanc's lake and stood by its edge. Behind her, hidden from view, waited the blacksmith with his chains, the mighty oxen and all the local men.

'Afanc, Afanc,' she called. 'Are you there? I'd love to see you.' There was nothing, only a light breeze ruffling the surface of the lake. She called again. 'Afanc? Come on my dear. Sit here with me.' This time the waters began to stir and swell, to bubble and boil. Siân started to sing, such a sweet voice echoing over the waters. The head of the monster emerged from the depths, water running down its face. 'Ah, you beautiful boy,' she said. 'Come and sit here with me.' And she sang more, charming the Afanc from the churning foam.

Slowly the frightful creature thrashed through the seething cauldron to the edge of the lake. The sight of its thick black hide, its snorting nostrils and sharp teeth would have caused a lesser person to run. But Siân stood still. As the dripping animal crawled from

the lake she sat down and sang. It dragged itself up to her and lowered its wet head to her lap. She reached a hand to its neck and gently stroked it, all the while singing a soft lullaby her mother had sung to her when she was a child. The mesmerized beast laid a giant claw on her shoulder and rested it there. Then it began to snore. It was ever thus. A gentle song and a sweet face can soothe the wildest beast.

Siân lifted her hand and signalled to the men hiding in wait. Quickly and quietly they set about binding the sleeping Afanc with the unbreakable iron chains. But the cold, clanking metal woke the slumbering monster. With a furious roar it leapt away from the maiden, tearing her breast with its sharp claw. It was the first sorrowful wound of the story. But the men had done their fastening work well and the Afanc's return to the lake came to a juddering halt. Under the guidance of Hu Gadarn the mighty oxen slowly heaved their burden out of the water and, with every man present lending his strength, dragged the poor Afanc from its home – the second sorrowful wound of the story.

They were heading for Llyn Ffynnon Las, a lake high in the mountains where they hoped the Afanc would do no harm. For many days they dragged the wretched creature up the rocky valley to where Dolwyddelan is today, over the shoulder of Moel Siabod (now known as the Hilly Pass of the Oxen) and into the Gwynant Valley. So great were the straining efforts of the oxen that the eye of one of them popped out. That place has since been called the Field of the Ox's Eye. The ox wept to lose his eye, his tears making a pool, which has ever after been known as the Pool of the Ox's Eye. And this is the third sorrowful wound of the story.

The mighty oxen struggled on until at last, below the sheer cliffs that drop directly from the summit of Yr Wyddfa, they came to Llyn Ffynnon Las, known today as Glaslyn. It is the highest lake in Wales. The exhausted oxen lay down to rest and the chains on the Afanc were loosed. It bounded into the deep blue lake to heal its bruises and to make itself a new home. And, if the story is to be believed, it is brooding there still. And the flooding in the Conwy Valley was never quite so bad again.

The Eagle and the Wren

Long ago the birds decided they needed a king. But how would they decide? Would it be the strongest bird, the fastest bird, the most beautiful bird or the wisest bird? After much bickering and twittering it was agreed that the King of the Birds would be the one who could fly highest in the sky. After all, flying is the one thing birds do best of all the creatures. So the highest flier would be their king.

The small birds – like Chaffinch, Robin, Blue Tit and Sparrow – weren't pleased because they knew they couldn't fly very high. But the birds of prey – Peregrine Falcon, Sparrow Hawk, Red Kite and Buzzard – thought they were in with a chance. But everyone knew that probably Golden Eagle would win. The funny thing was that Wren, the smallest of the birds, was hopping up and down going: 'Yes, yes, bird that can fly the highest in the sky, very good idea, very good idea!' They thought he must be daft in the head because the Wren can only fly as high as a bush.

The day came for the competition. All the birds gathered between the forest and the lake. There was much squawking, tweeting, croaking and chattering as they all got ready. They were about to begin when Wren, that cheeky little blighter, crept up behind Golden Eagle and, when no one was looking, hopped on to Eagle's back and disappeared into his neck feathers. And Wren was so light that Eagle didn't even know he was there.

Then they were off. There was a furious fluttering of feathers as into the air they flew. It wasn't long before the small birds – Chaffinch, Robin, Blue Tit and Sparrow – were dropping out of the race. But the middle-sized birds – Blackbird, Starling, Jay, Magpie, Woodpecker and Crow – were doing well. One tree high, two trees high, three trees high, but then, oh no, they too began to drop out of the race. Until finally the sky was left to the birds of prey.

Well not quite. Little Skylark was up there too, merrily singing herself higher and higher. Around her, rising and circling on warm currents of air, were Falcon, Hawk, Buzzard and Kite. But above them all was Golden Eagle. And slowly, one by one, the magnificent birds of prey and the joyous Skylark had to drop out until Golden Eagle was left alone, flying higher and yet higher.

By now Golden Eagle was so high he could see mountains and valleys, rivers and lakes, forests and fields, the sea and the islands across the sea … everything! But even Eagle has his limits and finally he could go no higher. He was about to begin his downward descent when Wren, that cheeky little blighter, hopped out of Eagle's neck feathers and flew – phut, phut, phut – above Eagle, about as high as a bush. 'What are you doing here?' cried Eagle angrily. But he was so tired he couldn't fly any higher. And so it was that Wren flew higher than any other bird!

Then Wren plummeted back to the earth. Eagle was so cross he swooped down trying to catch Wren. Just before they reached the ground Eagle came up behind Wren and swiped at him with his great beak, cutting off his back tail feathers. Ever since then Wren's tail has stuck up in the air and he's been called the 'Cut-Tail Wren' or the 'Cutty Wren' for short.

'Well?' clamoured the birds. 'Who went the highest?' Eagle had to admit that Wren had gone higher than him. The other birds thought it strange, but if that's what Eagle said then it must be true. And so they gave the crown for King of the Birds to … Wren!

But the next morning, after they'd had time to think about it, they realised that Wren must have cheated. Besides, they didn't want the smallest of the birds to be their king. So they stripped the crown from Wren and gave it to Golden Eagle. And Eagle went off huffing and puffing saying, 'Of course I should be the king!'

Then the birds decided that they were going to punish Wren – by drowning him in a bowl of tears. One by one they wept their tears of sorrow and the bowl got fuller and fuller. At last there was just one bird left to weep. Owl. Now Owl can be an ungainly bird, and as it walked up to the bowl one of its claws hooked over the edge and tipped it over, spilling all the precious tears onto the ground.

The birds were furious and cried, 'Owl! Owl! We don't want to see you again. You are banished to the night!' From that time on Owl has been a creature of the night. And if she ever comes out in the daylight the other birds will chase her away.

By now the birds didn't have any more tears to cry. They'd wept them all out. So they decided to let Wren off. Wren was very grateful to Owl and said, 'Of course Eagle should be the king, it was only a joke, only a joke'. But at least from that day on Wren could always say: 'Once I was King of the Birds, even if just for a day!'

The King with Horse 's Ears

Once upon a time there was a king who had a secret. His name was March and he had the ears of a horse! There are many versions of this story, many places that claim it as their own. This is the version told of the king whose castle was Castell March near Abersoch on the Llyn Peninsula in North Wales.

Because King March was embarrassed about his ears he used to wrap a cloth around his head and jam his crown down so no one could see them. No one knew the secret, not even his wife. Well, there was one person who knew, someone who got close to the king's ears once in a while. The barber. But the king said to the barber, 'If you ever tell anyone about my ears I'll have your head off in the morning!'

The barber didn't want to lose his head in the morning, or any other time for that matter, so he said nothing. But it's not so easy to keep a secret. The barber really wanted to tell someone. But he couldn't – for fear of losing his head. Soon that secret began to twist, tangle and tighten his stomach until he got the most terrible tummyache. Finally he could bear it no longer and went to see the doctor.

The doctor examined him – checked his pulse, his reflexes, looked into the pupils of his eyes – and finally said, 'The trouble with you is that you have a secret. And you're going to have to tell it to someone.'

'I can't,' said the barber. 'If I do I'll lose my head.'

'What you must do,' said the doctor, 'is tell your secret to the ground.'

'To the ground?' queried the barber.

'Yes, the ground,' said the doctor firmly.

So the next day the barber left the castle, went through the town, across the fields and into the forest. He walked and walked until he came to a clearing with a stream running through. He made sure no one was listening then he knelt down and whispered: 'King March has got horse's ears.' Afterwards he still had his head so he said it again a little louder. 'King March has got horse's ears.' He was starting to enjoy himself. He stood up and jumped up and down on the spot, chanting: 'King March has got horse's ears, King March has got horse's ears!' Ah, what a relief! The doctor had been right. He felt as if a great weight had lifted from his shoulders. He skipped and danced back to the castle and never gave the king's secret another thought.

But the ground has ears! And that night where he'd told his secret to the ground some tiny green shoots appeared. They grew and grew and in a short time were tall, strong, straight beautiful reeds, the finest in the whole of Wales.

A few days later a band of travelling minstrels was passing by on their way from the court of Maelgwn Gwynedd to perform for King March. They stopped in the middle of the forest for a picnic lunch and afterwards one of them went for a walk. That's how he came upon the tall, strong, straight, beautiful reeds, the finest in the whole of Wales. It so happened he was the piper and his pipes were made from reeds like these. So he cut a few of the best, went back to his friends and they spent the rest of the afternoon cutting, shaping, whittling and making a brand new set of pipes. Then they went on to King March's hall.

The tables were set for a fine banquet. People had gathered from near and far. When the feasting was over the king clapped his hands and called, 'Bring on the musicians, it's time for the dance!' The minstrels stepped forward. The piper stood with his brand new pipe. He was going to play the king's favourite tune. But when he put the pipe to his lips what should come out but: 'King March has got horse's ears, King March has got horse's ears!'

The king's face went red with embarrassment, then white with fury, then black with rage. He cried out: 'Throw them in the dungeons – I'll have their heads off in the morning!'

But the piper was a brave man. He stepped forward and said, 'Your majesty, it's not my fault. It's the pipe. It's bewitched.'

'Bewitched!' roared the king. 'Let me see!' He snatched the pipe and looked at it. It looked alright to him. Then he remembered he could play a tune on the pipe. But when he began playing his tune once again the pipe revealed: 'King March has got horse's ears, King March has got horse's …!'

Then he remembered the barber and the poor barber was dragged before the king. 'I'm sorry your majesty,' he blubbered. 'I just had a terrible stomachache and the doctor said I should tell the secret to the … to the … to the … ground. So I told the secret to the ground.'

'To the ground!' roared the king.

'Yes your majesty, to the ground.'

Then the whole story came out – how the barber had told the secret to the ground, how the reeds had grown up, how the piper had cut them and made a pipe and how it was the pipe that had told the secret. And by then it wasn't a secret. Everybody knew. But no one had laughed. Then someone at the back of the hall put up their hand and said, 'Excuse me your majesty. Could we see your ears?'

'You want to see my ears?' asked the king.

'Yes please your majesty.'

'Very well.' So the king took off his crown, unfurled the silken cloth and there were his beautiful horse's ears. He could twitch them just like a horse. In fact he had very good hearing. He could hear what was being whispered in the back of the hall, which is quite handy if you're the king.

He walked around the room showing off his ears and everyone gave him a polite round of applause. As he was the only king in the whole wide world with horse's ears and he was their king they were proud of him. And because they were proud of him, he was proud of himself. After that he never minded about having horse's ears and had a new crown made with two holes so his ears could poke through.

King March lived a good long life and when he finally died the story about 'the king with horse's ears' spread all the way around the world. And now they tell it in Ireland, North Africa, Eastern Europe, Greece, even as far away as India. But I like to think it's a story from Wales. And one more thing. If you have something unusual about you – it doesn't have to be horse's ears – anything that makes you different, don't be ashamed, be proud. Because remember. You are the only one of you there is!

The Drowning of Bala Lake

Bala Lake is the largest natural lake in Wales, 4 miles long and 1 mile wide. The River Dee runs into, through and out of it. Legend has it that the waters of the river and the lake do not mix! In Welsh it's known as Llyn Tegid, which some say means 'Lake of Serenity'. Whether or not that's the case, the truth is that once life in this valley was far from serene. For long ago, the story goes, there was no lake, just a broad, green, fertile valley. Nestling in the valley was the old town of Bala and next to the town, a grand palatial hall. But the lord and master of that hall was not a nice man. In fact, if the stories are to be believed, he was a nasty piece of work.

There are those who say this villain was none other than Tegid Foel, Tegid the Bald, husband to Ceridwen, worker of magic and mother, indirectly, of Taliesin. They say Tegid had grown embittered after his wife's failed attempt to gain favour and inspiration for their hideous son, Afagddu. So perhaps it was him, or perhaps it was some other scoundrel. Be that as it may, the lord of this Bala hall was an arrogant, greedy, heartless brute. The people in the valley had suffered greatly under his oppressive thumb. He was not a popular man. But he had money and power, so he called the shots. And one day, to celebrate the birth of his first grandson, he decided to hold a spectacular feast. All the greasy nobles and fawning sycophants in the region were invited.

On the afternoon of the feast the lord was walking in his garden when he heard a voice in his ear: 'Beware, beware, vengeance will come, vengeance will come.' It stopped him in his tracks. He looked around. No one was there. For a moment he puzzled, trying to make sense of it. Then he dismissed it from his mind as nonsense, a fault in his hearing, a glitch in his imagination.

That night the party raged. The tables were piled with succulent meats and aromatic delicacies. Barrels of ale and mead were tapped for the quaffing. As the lords and ladies talked loudly over each other and greedily stuffed themselves, outside the peasants shivered hungrily in their hovels. In between courses a harpist played. He was a mature man who had travelled far and was renowned for his repertoire and skill. He was also humble and not given to excess, so he was not impressed by the rowdy scene before him. But he was being paid for the night so he concentrated on making the best music he could in the circumstances. As the drink loosened their limbs the revellers danced.

Late in the evening there was a pause in the dancing. The harper was resting when suddenly a bird landed on his harp. It was a robin, its little red breast puffed out. He was startled, even more so when the bird spoke. 'Come away, come away,' it said. 'Vengeance will come, vengeance will come!' Then the bird flew a short distance off. The harper hesitated. This was crazy. Besides, he had tunes to play. But the bird came back and repeated its plea – 'Come away … vengeance …' – more forcefully than before. The harper looked around. At that moment no one was paying him any attention, so he rose to his feet and sidled after the robin. When he reached the door he stopped. What was he doing, following a bird? But the robin was back again, this time on his shoulder, repeating its message. He took one last look at the chaotic, noisy scenes in the hall and then slipped outside into the cool night air.

Cock Robin led him on, flying a short way ahead, then stopping and repeating its message. He walked after it, but when he reached the town gates he paused. He looked back at the distant hall, torches flickering in the windows, the sound of the revelry fainter now. 'What am I doing?' he thought, 'I haven't even been paid yet.' But the little bird was insistent. So he followed it in the moonlight, out of the valley and up the hill, across bogs, over streams, along a steep, narrow path through the trees. Eventually he reached the top of the hill and sat down to rest. He expected to hear the bird urging him on, but his fluttering, red-breasted companion had gone. There was nothing but the rippling murmur of a nearby

brook. He felt a fool and thought he should go back to the feast, at least to claim his precious harp. But by now the moon had set and without the bird to guide him he knew he'd never find his way in the dark. So he made a nest in the bracken and curled up to sleep.

As the sun rose over the Berwyn Mountains he woke, stretched and sat up. When he looked down the hill he couldn't believe his eyes. There was no great hall, no town, no fields. Instead a huge lake filled the valley, shimmering in the early morning sunlight. He was shocked and horrified. Then he remembered the robin that had led him away from impending doom. It had saved his life. It had been his guardian angel. He uttered a prayer of thanks to it then trotted off down the hillside to the lake edge. There was nothing, nothing at all to remind him of last night's festivity. Then he noticed something floating, drifting towards him on the glassy surface of the broad lake. He couldn't make it out at first. Then he knew. A surge of joy swept through him. It was his harp.

The Faithful   Hound

It is common to find different versions of the same story in far-flung parts of the world. But rarely can a story with such distant origins have been localised with such astonishing effect than the story of Gelert's Grave. It is likely that the original story was a Buddhist teaching tale from India. Somehow it made its way to South Wales and from there, by way of David Prichard, the hotelier charged with building the Goat Inn, it came to the small mountain village of Beddgelert in about 1801. Here the story truly found its home. Prichard told it to the poet William Robert Spencer who immortalised it in verse, thus ensuring that the tale spread far and wide. A grave was made to back up the story and thousands have been moved by it ever since. Perhaps it doesn't matter that it never actually happened in Beddgelert. It contains emotional and cultural truth and ultimately that's what really matters.

꩜

꩜

Gelert was Llywelyn's favourite hound. He was always ahead on the hunt, always first to the kill. His skill, speed and alertness were exhilarating. His master never hunted without him. Yet when Gelert was home he was as gentle as a lamb. He played with Llywelyn's one-year-old son so tenderly that one could easily think no one loved the little boy more.

One day Llywelyn and his wife Joan were staying in one of their summer homes up in the mountains. It was an unusual situation. Joan had to visit the local priest and the servants were all dispatched on various errands. Llywelyn readily agreed to look after their son himself for a couple of hours while everyone else was gone. All was going well when suddenly there was a baying of hounds and clatter of hooves outside the lodge. He opened the door. It was a group of his men going hunting. 'Will you join us?' they said. 'Come on. We're on the trail of a stag.'

'Er … well I can't,' replied Llywelyn. 'I'm … looking after the baby.'

Some of the men laughed. They didn't say it in his hearing but he knew they were thinking this was women's work and that he should be a man and join them on the hunt. He felt embarrassment and fury scorch his cheeks. When he turned back into the house he saw Gelert standing by the sleeping baby's cradle. He had an idea. Much as he loved to take Gelert on the chase, today Gelert could do a different job. Today he could look after the little boy. He spoke quickly to the hound, who clearly understood what he was to do. 'I won't be long,' he said, then leapt on his waiting horse and rode off with his men.

The hunt didn't go so well. They lost the stag, Llywelyn missed Gelert and maybe he felt slightly guilty that he'd left the boy with only the hound to look after him. Within the hour he was back at his lodge, down from his horse, with Gelert wagging his tail to greet him. He leant over to pat the dog then realised to his horror he was covered in blood. 'Oh no, what's happened?' he cried. He ran into the room where he son should be, only to see the cradle overturned. The baby's blankets were on the floor and there was blood everywhere. 'My son, my son, where are you?' His fear and his fury blinded him. He could not find the child anywhere.

Then he turned to his hound. 'Gelert, how could you? You beast!' In a fit of terror and rage he drew his sword and plunged it deep into the side of his faithful hound. As the poor dog let out his dying howl Llywelyn heard another sound. A crying infant. He ran over to the upturned cradle and there was his son, fresh-faced and rosy cheeked, just woken by Gelert's final yell. He picked up the boy and held him tight. Then he turned around and saw, behind the door where he had not looked before, the blood spattered carcass of a tremendous wolf. Only then did he realise what had happened. His beloved Gelert had saved his son, had protected him from the ravenous wolf. His bitter reward had been his master's sword.

What misery, what agony now filled Llywelyn's breast. He clasped Gelert's lifeless body to him but nothing could bring him back. Tears streamed down his face as he let loose his grief. When he had calmed a little he decided that the world should know of his folly and that his faithful hound would be honoured with a special grave for all to see. And so such a grave was indeed built and is visited by thousands still to this day.

As Spencer says in the last stanza of his poem, 'Beddgelert, or the Grave of the Greyhound':

> And, till great Snowdon's rocks grow old,
> And cease the storm to brave,
> The consecrated spot shall hold
> The name of 'Gelert's Grave'.

The Harp ist and the Key

In the hills above Trefriw in the Conwy Valley is an old farmhouse called Pencraig where long ago in the early sixteenth century lived William Owen and his wife Siân. They were a kind and generous couple and their home was often thrown open to people from near and far for feasts and fine entertainment. No one was ever turned away from their door. William was an excellent harp player and no evening was complete until he'd brought out his fine harp and played for the assembled company. His music was dearly loved and those who heard it were convinced that William played the sweetest tunes in the world. Some were his own compositions. One was particularly renowned and became known as the 'Conset of William Owen Pencraig'.

As well as being a farmer and a harpist, William was also a radical, agitating on behalf of independence for Wales. This was a dangerous thing to do at a time when the English Crown was seeking to suppress all signs of Welsh identity. One night word came to Pencraig that a small military force was heading that way and the rumour was they were out to arrest William Owen. Under cover of darkness William was forced to flee, taking nothing but a few survival essentials and leaving behind his beloved harp.

What happened to William Owen then is unknown. Some say he embarked on a sea voyage and that his ship was captured by pirates. For months he was stranded on a distant island. Others surmise that he was conscripted into the army against his will and forced to fight in foreign wars. But whatever it was, William was gone from Pencraig a long time. Gone too were the convivial gatherings that had taken place around the hearth there. No one played the great harp, which stood in the corner gathering dust. One year passed, then a second. Siân was worried that something terrible had happened to her dear husband and that she'd never see him again. Everyone in Trefriw and Llanrwst grieved for William. But there were some who saw this as an opportunity.

For Siân was still a beautiful woman and soon she was visited by men from the valley and beyond, begging her to marry again. Although her thoughts were always with the husband she loved, at last, after three years had passed, Siân agreed to marry the most convincing of her suitors. On the night before the wedding, Siân, with her husband-to-be, hosted a nuptial feast. It was the first time there had been such a gathering at Pencraig since William had hastily departed. After the supper some guests asked for a tune on the harp. One or two could play so William's old harp was taken from the corner and cleaned of dust and cobwebs. But no matter how they tried these harpists could only produced harsh, discordant sounds.

A little earlier in the evening, the maid had come to her mistress saying there was a stranger at the door, a shabby tramp who was asking for food and a bed for the night. As Pencraig was renowned for its generous hospitality Siân did not hesitate in giving permission for the man to be welcomed in and given food and drink. As he sat there eating in the kitchen he heard the tuneless and jarring noises coming from the harp next door.

'That harp needs tuning,' he said to the maid.

'There's no one in the house that can do it,' she replied.

'I can,' said the tramp. 'I was a harper once and have not forgotten.'

The maid told Siân and the tramp was sent for. He sat on a chair and carefully tuned the strings one by one. Then he began to play, sweeping his fingers lightly back and forth across the harp. The sweetest music filled the room. People stopped talking and turned to listen to the ragged man who was making the most wonderful sounds. Siân too looked. Something was stirring inside but she didn't yet know what. Then came a tune that she knew, and she knew that only one harpist in the world would know. The 'Conset of William Owen Pencraig'. It was her husband. He had come back.

Rather than rushing to greet her beloved she reflected for a few moments and came up with a plan. She went to speak to her betrothed and told him a story. She said that some time ago she had lost the key to Pencraig, a smooth and well-worn key she'd had for many years. Now she was thinking it was time to get a new key and was about to have one made. However, the old key had suddenly turned up and she thought it still fitted well. What should she do, she asked him? Use the old key or have a new one cut? He said that if the old key suited her better then of course she should stick to it and not bother with a new one. She said she would accept his advice.

As the strains of 'Conset' died away she went up to the harpist and introduced the luckless man to her husband. True husband and wife embraced and many tears of joy were shed. Word spread like wildfire around the house and the community and once again Pencraig was a place filled with music and wonder.

Rhys and Meinir at Nant Gwytheyrn

Two cousins – Rhys and Meinir Maredudd – became sweethearts. For weeks and months they courted each other, often meeting in the woods of Nant Gwytheyrn in the evenings. An old hollow oak was one of their favourite haunts. Meinir laughed as Rhys played his whistle. Rhys smiled as Meinir offered him bread and cheese. At last the time came for the two to be wed. The marriage was set to take place in the splendid church at Clynnog Fawr, just a few miles away from the Nant.

At that time it was traditional on the morning of the wedding for the bride to hide from the groom's friends who, when they found her, would escort her to the church. Rhys' friends set out to look for Meinir but they couldn't find her. For two hours they searched high and low but she eluded them. So they went on to the church, expecting to find her there. But she was nowhere to be seen.

Now anxiety turned to panic. The whole congregation went back to the Nant and spent the rest of the day looking. But she was not found, not that day nor on any other day in the weeks that followed. Poor Rhys was not just broken-hearted; he was maddened by his grief. He took to roaming about the valley, calling out to Meinir, sleeping among the roots of trees, forgetting about his family and his work. His only comfort was his faithful dog, Cidwm, who followed him everywhere.

One night months later, when Rhys was out aimlessly searching for his beloved, the wind picked up and the rain began lashing down. He and Cidwm took shelter from the storm beneath the old oak tree. Suddenly a bolt of lightning struck the tree and cracked the trunk open. Something fell crashing to the ground beside Rhys. He lit a match and screamed with terror when he saw that lying next to him was – a skeleton, covered with the tattered whisps of a wedding dress.

This was too much for poor Rhys. He literally died of fright there by the bony remains of his withered bride. And Cidwm, faithful to the end, lay down to sleep at his master's side and never woke up.

A Wedding in the Dark

Long ago a rich farmer and his wife lived in Cae'r Melwr near Llanrwst. They had one child, Elen, who was a pretty girl and the light of their lives. Nearby in a small cottage lived a poor widow who also had only one child, a lively, red-cheeked, mischievous boy called Jac. The two children played a lot together and Jac always had a great welcome at Cae'r Melwr.

When it came time for Elen to go to school in Llanrwst her father arranged for Jac to go too so the little girl would have company on her way back and forth to school. They travelled together like this for some years until Jac was old enough to leave school and get a job. He was taken on at Cae'r Melwr as a servant and there, over the years, proved himself to be such an able worker that by the age of 20 he was bailiff on the farm, much to the joy of his poor mother.

Elen was sent to a school in England to learn English and when she returned she was in the bloom of youth. By now Jac had learned everything on the farm and was thought of as the best farmer in the district, wise in the way of animals, land and business. His master, Elen's father, did not tire of praising him and asserted that he was the best lad from Chester to Conwy.

Elen and Jac were still great friends and she often went to the cottage to visit Jac's mother. People began to talk and the story spread that Elen and Jac loved each other. Some were even cheeky enough to ask the old man when his daughter was going to marry the manservant. But her father did not like this prospect and fell to brooding on the matter. One day he was at dinner with the squire of Gwydir Castle where he met an English gentleman who'd once visited Cae'r Melwr. He'd been very impressed by the orderly nature of this farm and said he'd pay a great deal to have Jac work as a bailiff for him.

At first the master didn't like the idea of his bailiff leaving, but then he realised it would be a way to separate Jac and Elen and put a stop to talk of their marriage. He spoke to his wife and though they were reluctant to lose a good bailiff, they desperately wanted their daughter to marry a gentleman. That could never be if she married a mere servant.

The next day Jac was told about the new job and agreed to it at once. Off he went and, though everyone else missed him, Elen never said a word about him. He sometimes wrote to his mother but never mentioned Elen. Elen's parents began to think there'd been no truth in the story about their daughter and Jac, and regretted letting the bailiff go.

Several years later the son of the Earl of Northampton came to stay at Gwydir Castle. One evening a dinner-dance was arranged at the castle and many young aristocrats from the area were invited, including Elen Cae'r Melwr. Of all the attractive young women present that night none could compare with Elen. The earl's son fell 'head over his ears' in love with her. Soon they were engaged and arrangements were begun for a wedding. Although everyone was excited about this forthcoming grand occasion, Elen herself was seldom seen outside the house. People thought it strange as they expected her to be happily preparing for her big day.

The day before the wedding the Earl of Northampton's son and his servants started early from Llangollen on fresh horses. He hadn't gone far when he met up with a dignified fellow riding in the same direction. After exchanging greetings the earl's son asked how far the stranger was going.

'To Capel Garmon near Llanrwst,' he replied.

'I'm going to Gwydir Castle just beyond Llanrwst,' said the bridegroom. 'Let's travel together to guard against thieves on this long and lonely journey.'

As they talked the earl's son said he was on his way to marry the loveliest girl in the land the very next day. After much chatter about himself he finally asked his co-traveller, 'But what about you? What's the purpose of your journey?'

'Oh,' said the stranger. 'I placed a snare behind me at the edge of the Conwy Valley and I'm going there now to see if I can raise it.'

The earl's son laughed at this odd response and thought his companion was just a little mad.

At the turning to Capel Garmon the two bade farewell and took leave of each other. As the earl's son went on to Gwydir the other rode to an inn near Capel Garmon. There he asked for a clergy-man and spoke intensely with him. The parson mentioned the big wedding at Gwydir Castle the next day. The mysterious fellow said he too wanted to marry the next morning, but very early, and that if the clergyman could arrange it he'd pay him handsomely in gold. The clergyman somehow overcame the usual rules and promised to conduct the wedding in the church at six in the morning.

The man left the inn for an hour or two and returned with a young lady. He left her there and went out again. This time he went to Cae'r Melwr and, though it was the dead of night, he woke the old man, who recognised Jac's voice at once. Jac said he was on an urgent errand and had come to beg a favour. The daughter of his master was with him and he wanted to marry her very early in the morning. 'Will you please come, my old master, to give away the young woman to your old lad.'

'I will come, my boy, with pleasure,' said the old man. He dressed and the two made off towards Capel Garmon.

The parson and the bellringer were waiting. The maidservant of the inn had agreed to be a bridesmaid and one of the men to be the best man. The marriage was conducted quickly with the old Cae'r Melwr man giving the bride away. He then wished the young couple every goodness and hurried home to prepare for the day's big wedding. He related these happenings to his wife, describing the beautiful girl Jac had for his wife but saying she was English and he hadn't seen her face properly in the dark church.

Soon Cae'r Melwr was bustling with preparations for the wedding. Six pretty bridesmaids were dressed in their best. It was a fine autumn day, the sun pouring its brilliant beams down on the place. At last it was time for Elen to appear, having dressed herself. But she did not come. Some of the maids went to her bedroom to look for her. She wasn't there! Everyone was shocked. Some wept with fear.

But after awhile the old man realised. 'I see how it is now. I gave away my own daughter this morning to be a wife for Jac.'

'Don't worry,' said his wife. 'Although she didn't have the son of an earl she had a man worthy of being called a man.'

The young couple were sent for to come home and great and warm was the welcome they had.

6

HISTORIC LEGENDS

The final tales in this book bring us to the realm of history. The lives of the earlier characters – Maelgwn, Gruffydd and Madog – though founded in fact, have been, to a degree, embellished with fiction. The stories of the two inspirational leaders, Llywelyn Fawr and Owain Glyndwr, are historically accurate but there was something superhuman about them which means they are remembered in Wales as legendary heroes. They did, after all, briefly succeed in uniting Cymru as an independent nation. The Red Bandits, Marged and Mari Jones were real enough but their stories have become the stuff of legend in Wales. And we conclude with the well-documented story of a tragic shipwreck on Anglesey in 1859, ending with a poignant twist.

Mael gwn, Dra gon of the Isle

> Oh thou dragon of the island … you are the first in mischief, exceeding many in power, and also in malice, more liberal than others in giving, more licentious in sinning, strong in arms, but stronger in working thine own soul's destruction. … Why dost thou show thyself unto the King of Kings … not better likewise in virtues than the rest; but on the contrary for thy sins much worse?

> Gildas, *On the Ruin of Britain*

Maelgwn Gwynedd, Hound Prince, Dragon of the Isle, was the ruler of North Wales in the early sixth century. He was an exceptionally powerful figure of a man and so was also known as Maelgwn Hir, Maelgwn the Tall. His great-grandfather, Cunedda Wledig, had come from Northern Britain, cleared the Irish from Ynys Môn and founded a dynasty there. By Maelgwn's time a court had been established at Aberffraw on the island, the traditional seat of power for the rulers of Gwynedd. This is why he was called the Dragon of the Isle. However, he is better known for having a castle at Deganwy near the mouth of the Conwy river.

Early in his career he abandoned his kingdom to become a monk, perhaps drawn in by the feeling that Christianity was the new and coming thing. Gildas (the Wise) in *On the Ruin of Britain* (written in about ad 540) says that Maelgwn had for his 'instructor the most eloquent master of almost all Britain'. He doesn't name him but it was probably Illtud, the founder of Britain's first ecclesiastical college in Llantwit Major – where Gildas himself was a student. However, Maelgwn soon found that a life of renunciation and piety wasn't for him. He revelled too much in the glories of battle, power, wealth and licentiousness. This was too much for the monk Gildas, who wrote with considerable vitriol of his former student friend:

> Maglocune, once thou didst ... vow thyself before God a monk with no intention to be unfaithful ... having ... (disavowed the) love of power, of gold and silver ... (and) the fancies of thine own heart ... Oh how great a joy should it have been to our mother church if the enemy of all mankind (the devil) had not lamentably pulled thee out of her bosom! Oh what abundant flame of heavenly hope would have been kindled in the hearts of desperate sinners, hadst thou remained in thy blessed state ... In short, thy conversion to righteousness gave as great joy to heaven and earth, as now thy detestable return, like a dog to its vomit, breedeth grief and lamentation ... Now thou dost not listen to the praises of God sweetly sounded forth by the pleasant voices of Christ's soldiers ...

but thine own praises rung out after the fashion of Bacchus's giddy
rout by the mouths of villainous followers, accompanied with lies
and malice ... so that the vessel prepared for the service of God is
now turned to a vessel of dirt ...

Gildas went on like this for several pages, singling out Maelgwn
for venomous vilification, but also tearing strips off four lesser
kings. Their crimes were essentially that they were un-Christian.
In Maelgwn's case his crime was aggravated because he had given up
the life of a monk, thus setting a bad example to others who might
be inclined to follow his lead. That's not to say he didn't deserve
at least some of the opprobrium. He did, allegedly, kill his wife
and nephew and marry his nephew's wife. But given that Gildas's
theme is 'ruin' he may well have been susceptible to exaggeration.
He does grudgingly acknowledge, if fleetingly, that Maelgwn was
'more liberal than others in giving'. Indeed he is supposed to have
supported many saints around Wales, including Saint Cybi on
Ynys Môn and Saint Padarn in Ceredigion. He is claimed as one
of the benefactors of the Diocese of Llandaff in its early years and
is also associated with the foundation of Bangor. So, despite his
many flaws, he tried to do good. Sceptics might say he was trying
to buy himself a place in heaven. Perhaps it was always thus.

One of the stranger stories told about Maelgwn is of how he
came to be pre-eminent among the kings of Britain. On Traeth
Maelgwn on the Dovey Estuary a contest was held to decide which
of the rulers of Wales should have supreme authority. They were
each to sit on their thrones on the beach and await the incoming tide. The one who could stay in place the longest would be
the High King. All the others had their heavy thrones dragged
onto the sand and were eventually forced to wade back through
the rising waters to save their lives. Maelgwn, however, instructed
the craftsman Maeldau Hynaf to make for him a chair of waxed
wings so that he alone could float above the surging sea and thus
be victorious.

Once established as High King at his court in Deganwy,
Maelgwn Gwynedd became a patron of the arts, especially music

and poetry. He kept a company of bards whose primary purpose –
according to Gildas and the Taliesin story that has come down
to us – was to exalt and honour their lord. Whether he was only
interested in hearing groveling sycophants singing his praises,
or whether he had a genuine interest in the arts, we shall never
know. But the picture passed down to posterity of Maelgwn
Gwynedd being pompously obsessed with his own self-importance
does seem something of a caricature. In reality it's likely that this
was only one facet of his passions.

It is said that Taliesin put a curse on Maelgwn Gwynedd.
He said: 'A wondrous beast shall come … to avenge the wrongs of
Maelgwn. Its hair and its teeth and its eyes shall be yellow, and this
beast shall be the end of Maelgwn Gwynedd.' And sure enough in
547 the plague of the Yellow Death was advancing across Europe
and at came at last to Gwynedd. In terror Maelgwn shut himself in
the church at Rhos near his court and ordered his guards to keep
all visitors away. He remained there a good while but one day he
heard his name being called and looked through a chink in the
church door. It was his fateful mistake. According to legend, at
that moment the plague, carried on the air, leapt through the hole
and into his body. Not long afterwards he was dead. But when
his men came to serve him food they saw him lying there and
thought he was asleep. They didn't want to disturb him so crept
away. Eventually they realised he could not still be asleep, and
found him dead in his bed. From that arose a proverb. When one
sleeps beyond measure or is dead it is 'the long sleep of Maelgwn in
the church at Rhos', being so long that there is no awakening. It's
thought that Maelgwn's body was buried on Ynys Seriol, or Puffin
Island, which stands off Ynys Môn near Penmon.

The picture that has come down of Maelgwn Gwynedd is that
he was a bloodthirsty buffoon. But much of what we know of him
is from the *Lives of the Saints*, which were composed many centuries after his death and were undoubtedly biased. Paradoxically
his role in these stories put him almost on a par with Arthur.
As Rachel Bromwich says, in her *Trioedd Ynys Prydein* (*The Triads
of Britain*):

In the Saints' Lives Maelgwn is portrayed as a typical *rex tyrannus* and acts as a foil to holy men in stories whose wide distribution over all parts of Wales is in itself highly suspect as evidence for their authenticity … In this capacity Maelgwn's prominence is rivalled only by that of Arthur. The names of both were borrowed by the ecclesiastical writers of the Lives from the secular tradition; and the implication would seem to be that in the eleventh century Maelgwn's fame as a heroic figure of earlier times stood out in a manner comparable with that of no other legendary character but that of Arthur himself.

Gruffydd the Wanderer

Hugh D'Avranches – also known as Hugh the Fat – was one of the Normans who fought at the Battle of Hastings with William the Conqueror. As his reward he was made Earl of Chester and given the freedom to claim North Wales. Ten years later, in 1076, he attacked Snowdonia.

At the time Gwynedd was in the hands of Gruffydd ap Cynan. He had been brought up in exile in Ireland and so was known as Gruffydd the Wanderer. When he returned from Ireland he brought with him Danes from Dublin and other Irish mercenaries. They were effective fighters with ferocious weapons, including two-headed axes and flails with sharp spikes which were like whirling scythes around the head.

In 1081 Hugh the Fat sent a message to Gruffydd inviting him to meet for a conference on the Conwy river, possibly where Gwydir Castle is today. But it was a trap. Gruffydd and his men were ambushed, his bodyguard was slain and Gruffydd was taken as a prisoner to Chester. Then the Normans took control of Gwynedd.

For twelve years Gruffydd was kept prisoner in Chester Castle. Occasionally he was taken from his cell and paraded in chains around the town to remind the Welsh that they were all now subject to their Norman masters. So it was that word got back to Snowdonia that their lord was still alive. Gruffydd himself kept his body fit by exercising constantly and kept his mind active by reciting from end to end the traditional stories he knew. Though he tried to escape many times he never succeeded.

Cynwrig the Tall was a strong young man who farmed with his brothers in the Snowdonian uplands. One day a traveller from Chester brought news of Gruffydd ap Cynan. Cynwrig became thoughtful. He asked his brothers about the family wealth and was told that it amounted to three pieces of gold. 'Then with three pieces of gold,' he said, 'I will purchase a nation.' And he set out for Chester with some sheep to sell.

He arrived, did his business, then wandered around the town. It happened that a feast was going on in the town hall. Gruffydd had been left with heavy chains on his arms and legs outside the door so that people could gawp at him. Cynwrig the Tall went up to him. Gruffydd recognised him as a Welshman at once and said, 'Tell the people of Gwynedd that Gruffydd the Wanderer is here and does not forget them.' He must have expected Cynwrig to stare and then walk away. But instead Cynwrig said, 'Come and tell them yourself!'

With that he bent over, picked up Gruffydd, threw him over his shoulders – chains and all – and began to run. People around were so stunned it took a while for the hue and cry to begin. But after a few streets the pursuers were catching up with the tall Welshman and his heavy load. So Cynwrig reached into his pouch and threw down the first piece of gold. The chasing men fell over themselves to grab it, giving Cynwrig time to reach the west gate of the city. But by then the chase was catching up again. So he threw down the second piece of gold and again gained precious seconds to make his escape. He was able to slip out of the gate and disappear into the woods. That night he used the last piece of gold to pay a blacksmith to cast off the chains.

Like a whisper of the winds through the grass the two men made their way back to Snowdonia and soon after the Welsh of Gwynedd threw off the Normans like a horse shaking off flies. It is said that when Hugh the Fat heard the news he had a fit that killed him. He left only a small son as Earl of Chester so for many years

the Welsh were left in peace. Until now the history of north-west Wales had been very turbulent, with different clans vying with each other for power. But now they'd learned about the dangers of the Norman threat they rallied around Gruffydd and he ruled Gwynedd for the rest of his life. He died in his bed, decrepit and blind, but still king at 70. No one had tried to depose him as they knew he represented freedom.

In the peace and strength of Gruffydd's rule Gwynedd prospered. People began planting orchards for the future rather than just their annual crops. They built stone structures hoping they would last. Gwynedd's villages filled with whitewashed churches that shone like stars. Gruffydd had a beautiful flaxen-haired wife who bore him seven children. Two of them became famous. His son, Owain, had his father's intelligence, courage and love of stories, and was an able poet. He became known as Owain Gruffydd and was a direct ancestor of the Llywelyns. His youngest daughter, Gwenllian, was also bright and brave, and shared her father's love of stories and their lands.

Gwenllian married Gruffydd ap Rhys, son of the last king of Deheubarth, who'd been killed by the Normans. Gruffydd was a freedom fighter and became known as the Red Fox. Giraldus Cambrensis told a story that at Llangorse Lake there were some special birds that would only sing on the command of the true king of South Wales. When the Normans had captured most of Brecknock, Gruffydd, the rightful king of the South, was walking with two Norman lords. Knowing this tradition the Normans called on the birds to sing. They stayed silent. Then Gruffydd, bowing to the birds and speaking to them solemnly, asked them to sing – which they did, and loudly.

But Gruffydd and Gwenllian were often forced to retreat from the Normans. So they set up a centre of resistance in the wild interior of mid-Wales at Cwrt-y-Cadno. Some say that it was in that court, in the 1120s and 1130s, that Gwenllian arranged for the 'Four Branches of the Mabinogion' to be written down for the first time, stories which had been remembered by Gruffydd the Wanderer in Chester Prison and passed onto his story-loving children.

Madog, Discoverer of America

Owain Gwynedd, son of Gruffydd ap Cynan, was Prince of Gwynedd in the twelfth century and regarded as one of the finest rulers of Wales in the Middle Ages. He had thirteen children from his two wives but another five born out of wedlock. Two of these were Madog, born in 1150 in Dolwyddelan Castle, and his brother Rhiryd. It was Welsh tradition at the time to acknowledge all children, including the illegitimate ones. However, when Owain died in December 1169 there was fierce rivalry between the eldest, Hywel, known as the Poet Prince, and his siblings. But Madog was a man of peace and found this squabbling tiresome. Besides, he'd heard a rumour through the Viking network that there was land beyond the great ocean that lay to the west of Ireland. 'I want to do something different with my life,' he thought. 'Come on Rhiryd, let's see if we can find that land!'

So, in 1170, 322 years before Christopher Columbus, he and his brother set sail into the complete unknown with two ships – the *Gorn Gwynant* and the *Pedr Sant* – and 100 companions. It's said they departed from the Afon Ganol in Penrhyn Bay. (There was no evidence of such a place until the 1950s when, during construction work on a new sea wall, the remains of a 1,000-year-old long-forgotten quay was found between Penrhyn Bay and Rhos on Sea.) Some months later, after being blown south into the Caribbean and up into the Gulf of Mexico, they made a landfall in a place that is thought to be where Mobile Bay, Alabama, is today. There Madog and his company disembarked.

The following year Madog returned to Wales with tales of the new country, warm, golden and fair. It seemed to fit with stories that had been told throughout the Celtic lands of islands to the west that were bountiful and blessed, where people never got old. Saints had told such stories. There was the Irish legend of Tir na Nog. Not surprisingly Madog was able to recruit more people to join him on his second voyage to this wondrous new land. It is said he headed west again, this time with ten ships. Whether they were blown off course and shipwrecked en route, or whether they happily settled and spent the rest of their lives in this 'promised land', no one will ever know. For Madog and his crew never returned.

However, some tantalising clues have been found, suggesting that Madog and his people did indeed settle in what is now America. Up the Alabama river are several stone fortifications unlike any other known Indian structure. In 1810 Jon Sevier, the first Governor of Tennessee, wrote a letter about a conversation he'd had in 1782 with the 90-year-old Cherokee, Oconostota, who'd been chief for nearly sixty years. The chief told him that it had been handed down by the forefathers that the forts were built by a white people who formerly inhabited the country. He'd heard his grandfather say they were called 'Welsh', and that they'd crossed the Great Water and landed first near the mouth of the Alabama river near Mobile. Their leader was called 'Modok'. Archaeologists testify that three major forts date to several hundred years before 1492. All are believed to have been built by the same group of people within a single generation. They bear a striking resemblance to the ancient fortifications of Wales. One is almost identical in setting, layout and method of construction as Dolwyddelan Castle in Gwynedd, the presumed birthplace of Madog. Sevier also said that six skeletons had been discovered in brass armor bearing Welsh coat of arms.

The situation of the forts, blended with the accounts given by the Indians of the area, has led to a plausible reconstruction of the trail of Madoc's colonists. The settlers would have travelled up the Alabama river and secured themselves at the Lookout Mountain site, which took months, maybe years to complete. It is presumed the hostility of the Indians forced them to move on up the Coosa river, where the next stronghold was established at Fort Mountain, Georgia. Situated atop a 3,000ft mountain, this structure had a main defensive wall 855ft long, and appears to have been more hastily constructed than the previous fort. Having retreated from Fort Mountain, the settlers then built a series of minor fortifications in the Chattanooga area, before moving north to the forks of the Duck river (near what is now Manchester, Tennessee), and their final citadel, Old Stone Fort. Formed by high bluffs and 20ft walls of stone, Old Stone Fort's 50 acres was also protected by a moat 1,200ft long. Like the other two major defense works, Old Stone Fort exhibits engineering proficiency not found in native America.

Early explorers found evidence of possible Welsh influence among the indigenous peoples much further north along the

Tennessee and Missouri rivers. In the eighteenth century one tribe was discovered that seemed different to the others that had been encountered before. Called the Mandans they were described as white men with forts, towns and permanent villages laid out in streets and squares. They claimed ancestry with the Welsh and spoke a language remarkably similar to it. Instead of canoes, Mandans fished from coracles, an ancient type of boat still found in Wales today. Unlike members of other tribes, these people grew white-haired with age. George Catlin, a nineteenth-century painter who spent eight years living among native tribes including the Mandans, believed he'd found the descendants of Madog's expedition. He speculated that the Welshmen had lived among the Mandans for generations, intermarrying until their two cultures became indistinguishable. Unfortunately the Mandans were virtually wiped out by a smallpox epidemic introduced by traders in 1837.

The story of Madog's voyage was used during the reign of Elizabeth I as an attempt to prove prior discovery of the North American continent by Great Britain in order to lay claim to the New World. Some have therefore dismissed it as a story invented purely for that purpose. However, one of the earliest accounts of the tale was written by Gutyn Owen, a renowned Welsh historian and genealogist, whose book was published before 1492, therefore refuting that idea. Clearly it is a story that was handed down by word of mouth for many generations before that.

The belief in Madog's voyage to America and his settling among the native peoples continued into the twentieth century. In 1953 a plaque was placed at Mobile Bay by the 'Daughters of the American Revolution'. It read: 'In memory of Prince Madog, a Welsh explorer who landed on the shores of Mobile Bay in 1170 and left behind, with the Indians, the Welsh language.' However, the plaque did not last long and was removed by the Alabama Parks Department. After all, Madog's landing, if it happened, did not result in the conquest of the Native America by the European nations. Rather it led only to a relatively peaceful assimilation into it. Madog was a man of peace after all.

Llywelyn Fawr and Siwan

Llywelyn ap Iorweth, born in 1173, was a precocious lad. According to Giraldus Cambrensis he was only 12 when he embarked on a series of battles to wrest the rulership of Gwynedd from his two uncles, Rhodri and Dafydd. With the help of two cousins and his uncle Rhodri, Llywelyn first expelled Dafydd from Gwynedd east of the Conwy river. Then he turned on his erstwhile ally, Rhodri – who controlled the land to the west of the Conwy – and defeated him. After this he focused on overcoming his cousins. This was how it was in those days. Family feuding was the order of the day. Internecine rivalry was rife. Clearly Llywelyn was determined and ambitious from an early age. Perhaps he had a sense of destiny. By the time he was 25 he was the sole ruler of Gwynedd.

Although Tangwystl was never his wife, she was, around this time, the mother of Llywelyn's first son, Gruffydd. (Though he was illegitimate Gruffydd played a key role in events over the following decades and ironically it was his son Llywelyn who later carried the mantle of his illustrious grandfather.) By the early 1200s Llywelyn was calling himself the Prince of North Wales and was keen to establish his dominance over other Welsh princes. In time he surged down into Powys and Deheubarth and exerted his power and authority there.

On the eve of Llywelyn's ascendancy Wales was predominantly a land of pastoral warrior tribesmen who survived by keeping cattle and sheep, supplementing this with hunting, gathering and fishing. As Giraldus said, the people ate 'more flesh than bread'. Their isolated settlements lay far apart, separated by long stretches of rough moorland and steep, wooded valleys. This meant people's lives were dominated by local patriotism and fierce family loyalties which led to blood feuds. The physical barriers, which kept clans apart, helped to perpetuate a fragmented political system with numerous mutually hostile chieftains. Matters were made worse by the age-old custom of divided succession among the sons of a deceased ruler. It led to frequent fratricidal conflict.

Llywelyn was broadminded enough to recognise that there were lessons to be learned from the changing concepts and methods in Norman England. He introduced the practice of primogeniture – the right of the first-born son to inherit all the estate rather than it being split among other offspring – hoping that this would reduce familial strife. He made individuals responsible for criminal acts rather than the family as a whole. He also encouraged the building of market centres and ports, and along with that came the construction of better dwellings and greater cultivation of the fields.

Llywelyn also realised that to support his position in Wales vis-à-vis other Welsh princes he would need to enter into a relationship with King John of England. In 1201 the two of them agreed a treaty – the first of its kind between a Welsh prince and an English king – whereby Llywelyn swore fealty to John and undertook to pay him homage in exchange for maintaining his title as Prince of North Wales. But that wasn't the only thing that was to bind them together. Four years later Llywelyn married Joan, King John's illegitimate daughter. Joan, or Siwan as she was called in Wales, was an unusual princess. Her grandmother had been the spirited and highly intelligent Eleanor of Aquitane, who was reputed to have held the Court of Love in Poitiers. Siwan herself was brought up in France with this lively, literary family, where love and the rights of women were prominent. When she was betrothed to Llywelyn ap Iorweth some, in France at least, must have doubted her luck.

But Llywelyn was no ordinary leader and relished the chance to inject some European flair into his courts at Aberffraw and Abergwyngrgyn. Siwan fitted in perfectly with these ambitions. She was responsible for running the courts when Llywelyn and his army were away. At times she also played a key diplomatic role – often between her husband and her father. In the first few years of their marriage Llywelyn and his father-in-law, King John, were allies. Llywelyn even joined him in a military campaign against William the Lion, King of Scotland. But in 1210 relations soured when Llywelyn supported the Marcher lord, William de Braose, whom John had declared a traitor. After a failed first attempt, in the late summer of 1211 King John marched with his army across North Wales as far as Bangor, where the town and the cathedral were mercilessly ravaged. It was the first time a Norman army had penetrated the Welsh heartland west of the Conwy river. The bishop, taking sanctuary in his church, was dragged from the blazing building, later being ransomed for 200 hawks. All this forced Llywelyn to negotiate. He sent Siwan to parley with her father, but even with her tactful intervention the price John demanded for peace was crippling: 20,000 head of cattle and all the lands east of the Conwy river. Llywelyn was also forced to give up his son Gruffydd, son of Tangwystl, as a hostage to the king. He was, however, left with the title of Prince of Gwynedd.

Paradoxically this pressure from King John drove other Welsh princes from Powys and further south, who'd previously sided with the king, into alliances with Llywelyn. Impressed by his statesman-like leadership, they, along with some Marcher lords, followed him in a campaign against John. In 1212 Llywelyn was the first Welsh prince to conclude a treaty of alliance with a foreign power, the king of France. He also persuaded the Pope, Innocent III, to absolve him from his oaths of fealty to King John. This tide of feeling against King John lifted the English barons who took London and forced him, in 1215, to sign Magna Carta. In it land taken in Wales was to be restored to the rightful owners and Welsh law was to have primacy in Wales once again. Llywelyn, mentioned by name in the text, was to have his son returned and all other hostages would be released.

Buoyed by this turn of events Llywelyn summoned the other princes of Wales to a meeting in Aberdyfi in 1216. There he extracted oaths of homage and obedience from them all, a clear demonstration of his authority. In effect he diverted the allegiance of these lords from the Crown to himself, meaning he was now in control of a large part of Wales. He became known by the resounding title of 'Prince of North Wales and Lord of Snowdonia'. He won the loyalty of those chiefs who acknowledged his overlord-ship and brought independent Wales to a high point in her history.

Llywelyn's political success was marred in later life by a personal tragedy. In 1228 he captured another William de Braose, grandson of the one who'd once been his ally, in a battle near Montgomery.

The captive was brought back to the court at Aber to be ransomed – for £2,000. At that time marriage was a primary act of alliance between political adversaries, so in negotiation William agreed that one of his daughters, Isabella, would marry Dafydd, Llywelyn's son by Siwan and his legitimate heir. So far so good. But William was wounded when brought to Aber. He needed someone to care for him. He didn't speak Welsh. His first language was French, as was Siwan's. So it is likely that she tended his wounds and nursed him back to health. As she did so they must have talked. Perhaps he brought into her life some of the romance and glamour associated with the French court. Perhaps this, and her tender touch, drew them together. In time their friendship became intimate and they embarked on a secret affair.

At Easter 1230 de Braose visited the court at Aber to finalise his daughter's wedding arrangements. And … to see Siwan. One fateful night he was found, presumably in flagrante, with Siwan in Llywelyn's chamber. Such behaviour may have been acceptable in the court at Poitiers but it was not in the courts of Gwynedd. It's possible someone ensured they were caught to make Llywelyn look like a fool and to weaken his power. However it happened, it wasn't long before everyone knew of the scandal. Llywelyn's council decided there was only one response to this offence. William would hang and Siwan would be imprisoned. These punishments were duly carried out.

Siwan was effectively under house arrest for a year. But Llywelyn clearly loved her and after that time found it in his heart to forgive her. So she was released from prison and reinstated as his wife. When she died in 1237 she was buried on Anglesey in a place Llywelyn could see from his court in Aber. He built a priory there at his own expense, for, it was said, 'the soul of his lady'.

Llywelyn was very keen that Dafydd, his son with Siwan, be his legitimate heir and went to considerable lengths to ensure it, even petitioning the Pope to have Siwan recognised as a legitimate daughter of King John. Although his eldest son Gruffydd was given land – mainly the Llyn and Meirionydd – he was imprisoned by his father between 1228 and 1234 because he was regarded as not being up to the job. Llywelyn suffered a stroke soon after Siwan's death and from that time on Dafydd took an increasing part in ruling the principality. Llywelyn died in April 1240 in the Cistercian abbey at Aberconwy where he was buried. When Edward I later built Conwy Castle on the site the abbey was moved a few miles up the river to Maenan. Llywelyn was reburied there and his remains remained there until the Dissolution of the Monasteries, at which point his bones and the coffin were unceremoniously thrown into the river. The stone sarcophagus was retrieved, however, and now rests in Llanrwst church.

After Llywelyn's death Dafydd took over his father's title. However, his conflict with his half-brother Gruffydd continued and eventually Dafydd was obliged to hand over Gruffydd to King Henry III as a hostage and part of a treaty which restricted his power. Gruffydd was killed trying to escape from the Tower of London in 1244. Dafydd himself was dead two years later, having left no heir. Paradoxically it was Gruffydd's son Llywelyn who later took on the mantle of Prince of Wales and who was the second of the famous Llywelyns. However, he became known as Llywelyn the Last as his only daughter, Gwenllian, was placed in a nunnery by the English Crown and never had any children. The royal line of Gwynedd was thereby extinguished with Llywelyn's death.

Llywelyn ap Iorweth dominated Wales for more than forty years. Though many of his achievements collapsed within fifty years of his death, he came closer than any other ruler to bringing about a unified and independent Wales. He was a strong leader with a civilising influence. He encouraged cultivation and building. He disapproved of pillaging after battle. He constructed several castles, including Castell y Bere, Dolwyddelan and Dolbadarn near Llanberis, which guarded the main way into the mountains. He was a generous supporter of the Church, providing grants of land for the building of monasteries. And he was a patron of Welsh culture. Many of the poets eulogised him. It was left to an English monk, however, to accord him his most lasting epithet. Matthew Paris, a contemporary of Llywelyn, was the first to describe him as 'great'. Ever since then he has been remembered as Llywelyn Fawr, Llywelyn the Great, an accolade awarded to only one other Welsh leader, Rhodri Fawr (ad 820–878). He was indeed a man of destiny.

Owain Glyndŵr's War of Independence

There is a long tradition in Britain of prophets forseeing the coming of a deliverer who will rise up and rid the land of the hated invader, restoring peace and justice to a united people. One of the earliest such prophecies is attributed to Merlin who, in the fifth century, foresaw the coming of a noble king who would restore harmony and give rise to tales that would be 'as meat and drink to the storytellers who relate them in ages to come'. He was, it seems, referring to Arthur. However, when his rambling prophecy was transcribed by Geoffrey of Monmouth in 1136 it became ripe

William Blake's 'visionary' head of Owain Glyndŵr. (Wikimedia Commons)

for reinterpretation. In the early 1400s the Welsh bards had no qualms about seizing upon it and applying it to their new saviour. For Wales now needed a national redeemer who would drive out the invading Normans and return the country to its former glory. As Geraldis Cambrensis had written two centuries before: 'The English fight for power, the Welsh for liberty; the one to procure gain, the other to avoid loss ...' Owain Glyndŵr (born in 1349 or 1359) did not shrink from stepping into this role of 'y mab darogan', 'son of prophecy'. He was determined to lead his compatriots to liberty.

Glyndŵr was from the uchelwyr, the Welsh nobility, who had generally adopted loyalty to the Crown and its Marcher barons in return for secure tenancy on their hereditary estates. But they suffered heavy taxation, were often legally discriminated against and knew their lands had been taken from them by force. They could see the Normans were attempting a creeping takeover of Wales and had a growing feeling of enough is enough – 'this far and no further'. The Norman practice of seizing Welsh land affected Glyndŵr directly. When Reginald de Grey, Lord Grey of Ruthin, first tried to appropriate some of his land, the Welshman took his grievance to the court of Richard II. As a young man Owain had studied law for seven years at the Inns of Court in London so he knew his way around. He had contacts and allies and the king found in his favour. But Grey then embarked on a campaign to undermine Glyndŵr in the eyes of the English law. He sent letters to the Prince of Wales implicating Glyndŵr in the activities of a bandit at large on Grey's estate. Glyndŵr repudiated this charge and again took his case to London. But by now Richard II had been usurped by Henry Bolingbroke, who, as Henry IV, was less sympathetic to Glyndŵr's cause. This time his case was thrown out with the words: 'What care we for these barefoot Welsh dogs?' Not only that, Parliament insisted that Glyndŵr offer Lord Grey further concessions.

Soon after the new king summoned Owain Glyndŵr to join a general muster for a campaign to Scotland. Lord Grey was in charge of enforcing such royal commands in the northern marches but did not inform Glyndŵr of it until the day before. So it was impossible for Glyndwr to comply with the order or even explain his absence. Failure to respond to the king's order was deemed treason and Glyndwr's estates could now be forfeited. On returning from Scotland, Grey invited Glyndwr to a reconciliation meeting. It was early September 1400. Glyndwr knew Grey could not be trusted and insisted the meeting take place at his court at Glyndyfrdwy. Grey was to bring no more than thirty armed men. But after the Lord of Ruthin set out a separate party of heavily armed horsemen followed behind him, dispersing in the woodland around Glyndwr's manor. They were joined by another large force under Earl Talbot from Chirk. Fortunately they were spotted by Glyndwr's bard, Iolo Goch, who alerted his master with a spontaneously composed englyn. Glyndwr made a narrow escape (the first of many) but was forced to go into hiding, confirming himself as a traitor in English eyes. Glyndwr now decided he would have no justice from the English Crown and that his life would be always in danger. So, on 16 September 1400, having escaped Grey's trap, in the presence of friends, family, poets and priests, Glyndwr was proclaimed Prince of Wales at his court in Carrog. According to Welsh law he was perfectly suited for the position as he was descended through his father from the kings of Powys and through his mother from the royal line of Deheubarth. He also had family links to the old kingdom of Gwynedd. On that day he raised the standard of the Golden Dragon and began his war of independence. Soon thousands were flocking to join him.

The first act of his rag-tag force was to burn down Grey's town of Ruthin. Then followed the burning of many Anglo-Norman boroughs including Denbigh, Flint, Oswestry and Welshpool. Glyndwr sought to avoid pitched battle, as his supporters were not well armed. Rather he engaged in guerilla tactics, attacking and burning towns then melting back into the hills with the spoils of war. His fighters wore little armour and rode light horses. They had few swordsmen but many good bowmen. Indeed, Wales was the original home of the most formidable infantry weapon, the 6ft longbow. This meant that they were ideally suited for mobility and surprise. Ambush was a key tactic. The armour of the

English became a disadvantage, weighing them down and slowing them up. Glyndwr's men had the weather in their favour too. They were used to wind and rain and knew the land well. Indeed, so often was the weather on Glyndwr's side it was rumoured he had wizard-like powers over the elements.

The bards swiftly spread the news of Glyndwr's uprising across Wales, no doubt embellishing as they did. As a consequence the Commons in London grimly passed a law banning them, determined to suppress 'wasters and rhymers, minstrels and vagabonds ... whom by their divinations, dreams and excitations draw the Welsh into insurrection and rebellion'. Not only that, the rights of Welshmen were severely curtailed. They were forbidden from purchasing land near the Marcher towns and from marrying English people. No Welshman was allowed to be a JP, chief forester, chancellor or constable of a castle. All these posts were immediately given to Englishmen. From now on the Welsh were to be collectively responsible for any damage which occurred in the course of the war. And all court proceedings were to be in what was, for them, a foreign language: English. These and similar edicts meant that the Cymru had nothing to lose by joining Glyndwr. Welsh labourers working in England and Welsh students at Oxford University returned to Wales to join their countrymen.

Over the following twelve years Henry IV and his son Prince Hal launched six punitive expeditions into Wales in an attempt to crush Glyndwr's revolt. On the first such attack in late September 1400 the new king sped across North Wales from Shrewsbury to Bangor, sacking, burning and looting as far as Harlech. This method of laying waste (known as *chevanchée*) was used on all subsequent expeditions. On Anglesey eight Welshman were executed without trial. One, said to be involved in the original attack on Ruthin, was hung, drawn and quartered and the quarters of his body were sent to Bristol, Hereford, Ludlow and Chester as a warning to the Welsh. After this initial onslaught Owain and many of his followers retreated into the safety of Snowdonia. The English authorities assumed their rapid and firm response had nipped the revolt in the bud. Pardons were offered to all Welshmen who submitted.

However, the following year widespread starvation and continued English oppression fuelled renewed support for Glyndŵr's rebellion. On 1 April 1401 a company of just forty men, led by Rhys and Gwilym ap Tudor from Anglesey, tricked their way into the supposedly impregnable Conwy Castle. They knew that on Good Friday the small garrison of men-at-arms and archers would be at prayer in the parish church. The story goes that one of Glyndŵr's supporters walked into the castle disguised as a carpenter, his toolbox concealing hidden weapons. Once inside he strangled the two unsuspecting guards on the gate and let the war party in. They quickly overcame the remaining guards and took control of the mighty fortress. The town was set ablaze, alerting the constable and his men, but they were unable to retake the castle. Meanwhile the Welsh burned all the records of the town's exchequer. Although Rhys and Gwilym eventually gave up Conwy Castle in exchange for pardons, soon after there were further uprisings, not just in the north, but also in Powys, Cardigan, Brecon and Carmarthenshire. The whole of Wales was rallying to Glyndŵr's cause.

Inevitably there was an ebb and flow to Glyndŵr's fortunes. Things often went quiet in the winter months, only to rise up again in the spring. In early 1402 a blazing comet appeared in the sky which the bards interpreted as an omen favourable to Glyndŵr. Then in mid-April Owain and his men went again to attack Ruthin Castle. After being initially repulsed they withdrew out of bowshot range. Reginald de Grey, probably urged on by Glyndŵr sympathisers, led a charge from the castle to finally vanquish his foe. Glyndŵr rode off with Grey in hot pursuit. Then the Normans saw a huge force waiting for them in the woods. They wheeled around to escape but fell straight into a Welsh ambush. The 'huge force' was no more than captured cloaks and helmets set on poles! Grey's return to the safety of the castle was now cut off and he was surrounded by archers. He and six of his bodyguard made it to Bryn Saith Marchog, the Hill of the Seven Knights. Most of his men were killed but Grey himself was more valuable alive. He was captured, taken to Dolbadarn Castle at the foot of Snowdon and imprisoned there for a year. A ransom was set of 11,000 marks.

Eventually this was paid by Henry IV but repaying the debt led
to Grey's financial ruin. And he had to swear never to bear arms
against Glyndŵr again.

Soon after this Glyndŵr's forces achieved another success.
They encountered the army of Sir Edmund Mortimer at Bryn
Glas near Knighton in the borderlands. Because of the shape
of the hill Owain was able to hide half of his men in a wooded
hollow. Also there were Welsh longbowmen within the ranks of
the English army with a secret allegiance to Glyndŵr. Mortimer's
men were struggling to make headway uphill when Glyndŵr's
banner appeared. At that moment his men emerged from cover
to attack and the Welsh longbowmen switched sides. The English
battling on the hill were decimated and Mortimer and several of
his companions were captured. This was the first time the Welsh
had won a victory in open battle against the English.

Glyndŵr hoped to extract a higher ransom for Mortimer than
for Grey. But Mortimer's young nephew had a stronger claim to
the English throne than Henry and the king was wary of him.
He refused to pay the ransom and instead imposed massive fines
on the Marches as a punishment for border Welshmen helping
Glyndŵr. However, throughout Wales fines and rents went unpaid.
As more men thronged to support Glyndŵr's war of independence, garrisons were placed on high alert. The rebel army swept
through the south, assaulting and burning the castles at Usk,
Abergavenny, Caerleon, Newport and Cardiff. Aware that, in the
Vale of Glamorgan, he was vulnerable to the already mustering
English armies, Glyndŵr then headed west, attacking Aberystwyth,
Harlech and Caernarfon castles before making his way back to
his homeland in north-east Wales. In September 1402 Henry IV
began a three-pronged attack on Wales from Chester, Shrewsbury
and Hereford. The king himself led a force from Shrewsbury and
destroyed the market town of Llanrwst, slaughtering all its inhabitants. But Glyndŵr must have used his 'magical powers' to direct
the weather. On 7 September a tornado tore through the country,
blowing away the English army's tents. Henry would have been
crushed to death by a giant tent pole if he'd not been sleeping in

his armour. His army returned to England humiliated and in dis-array. Whether or not Owain had power over the elements matters not. The English, at least, believed he did.

Later in 1402 Edmund Mortimer, now an ally of Glyndŵr, married Owain's daughter, Catrin. Meanwhile Henry Percy, Earl of Northumberland, and his son 'Hotspur', had been repelling a Scottish incursion along the border. They captured five Scottish earls but Henry IV ordered that they should not be ransomed. This angered the Percys and led to them falling out with the king. Soon after they had discussions with Mortimer and Glyndŵr and switched sides to support the Welsh war. In 1403 Glyndŵr con-solidated his power base in the upland areas of north-west Wales. The English castles of Beaumaris, Caernarfon and Harlech were now beleaguered outposts, surviving only because they could be supplied from the sea. But Prince Hal (later Henry V), though only 16 years old, led an army into the north and destroyed Sycherth and Glyndyfrdwy, Glyndŵr's ancestral homes. Despite this Owain was on the ascendant. In July that year there was a general uprising in the Tywi Valley and Owain himself led a tri-umphant army down the valley, taking the castles of Dryslwyn, Newcastle Emlyn and Carmarthen along the way. At the same time Hotspur led the revolt in north-east Wales, though he was killed in the Battle of Shrewsbury later that month. Prince Hal himself was seriously wounded. Nonetheless in the summer of 1403 there was virtually no part of Wales untouched by the flame of rebellion. In November, with the help of Glyndŵr's new allies the French, Caernarfon Castle was under siege, along with all the other castles in north-west Wales. For Henry IV the situation did not look good.

In spring 1404 a French naval blockade at Harlech Castle starved out the garrison, forcing them to surrender. Glyndŵr swiftly moved in and made it his family home. It was also to be his court and military headquarters for the next four years. Soon after he held his first Parliament or Cynulliad (gathering) of all Wales in Machynlleth. Before a vast assembly that included senior church-men and envoys from Scotland, France and Castile, Glyndŵr was crowned 'Owain IV, Prince of Wales'. Missives were sent to France to establish a treaty and Owain set out his vision for an independent Wales. It was to have a regular Senedd and an independent church. He wanted two national universities, one in the north and one in the south, and a return to the traditional and more equitable laws of Hywel Dda. The following year, after discreet negotiations (led by Welsh bishops), the Tripartite Indenture was signed in Bangor. This was an agreement between Owain Glyndwr, Edmund Mortimer and Henry Percy, Earl of Northumberland, to divide England and Wales into three parts. Wales would extend as far as the rivers Severn and Mersey and include most of Cheshire, Shropshire and Herefordshire. The Mortimers would take all of southern and western England, and Thomas Percy would have northern England as far south as Leicester and Norfolk. Through marriage all three parties had a share of a legitimate claim to the throne of England. The parliament and this agreement represent the high point of Glyndwr's war of independence.

For two years the French supported the Welsh insurgency, mainly through a series of raids on English harbours. However, in August 1405 a French force landed at Milford Haven. Some 5,000 French were joined by 10,000 Welsh under Glyndwr and they marched across South Wales through Herefordshire to Worcester. There they took up a position on Woodbury Hill. Soon after Henry IV arrived with his army and camped on another hill a mile away. There were skirmishes between raiding parties but an impasse between the two main armies. After eight days Henry retreated overnight into Worcester and shortly afterwards the Welsh and French withdrew back through Wales. Within a year the French had withdrawn their support for Glyndwr's campaign due to political changes in Paris and a new desire for peace with England. At the same time Glyndwr found that his Scottish allies had been made ineffective by the capture of their king. Now Owain was on his own against an enemy with far more resources than him. At the time the population of Wales was 150,000 and that of England over 2 million. In 1407–08 there was an uncommonly severe winter making it even harder for Glyndwr to feed his men and horses. His support was slipping away.

By now the English had also changed their strategy. Rather than focusing on the punitive expeditions favoured by Henry IV, Prince Henry, now more experienced and a better leader than his father, concentrated on economic blockade. He eventually captured Anglesey, the traditional 'bread-basket' of North Wales. He strengthened the castles that remained in English control and, by cutting off trade and the supply of weapons, gradually retook Wales. In September 1408, after sixteen months of bombardment, Aberystwyth Castle fell to the English. And finally, in February 1409, after a prolonged siege under the command of Prince Henry, Harlech Castle was retaken by the English. Lord Edmund Mortimer had already died during the winter. Owain's wife Marged, along with his daughter Catrin (Mortimer's widow) and four of her children were taken as prisoners to the Tower of London where they all died before 1415. Glyndwr himself escaped. Some say he disguised himself as an elderly peasant and slipped unnoticed through the English ranks.

Once again Owain Glyndwr, master of escape, was on the run. It was then he vanished into the mountains to the home of his friend, Rhys Goch Eryri, above Beddgelert on the flanks of Moel Hebog. But word got out that Red Rhys had a distinguished guest and one day a party of armed soldiers was seen approaching the house. Owain and Rhys ran out the back door in servants' clothes. Rhys tried to draw the soldiers after him and away from Owain, but when his hat blew off revealing his red hair the soldiers turned their chase to the other fleeing figure. Owain was making for Aberglaslyn and the sea but his escape was cut off by men-at-arms. So he turned back to the mountain. His pursuers were almost within bowshot as he ran up the steep hill toward a pass that offered a safe way through. Suddenly he heard a triumphant yell and saw his route blocked by half a dozen soldiers. He turned to the cliffs that hemmed him in. The vertical precipice was split by a cleft nearly 300ft from top to bottom. This was his only chance of escape. He scrambled up the scree then threw himself at the rock. It was a tough climb but there were just enough foot and hand holds for him to make his ascent. None of the soldiers dared to follow him. Instead they trudged off to gain the crest by an easier way. But when they reached it there was no sign of Owain. Believing he'd fled down into Cwm Pennant beyond the mountain, they spent the rest of the day searching there. But they looked in vain for, after emerging from the top of his chimney, Owain had run along the ridge and down into a hidden cave. There he stayed for six months, being secretly provisioned by the abbot from Beddgelert Priory. The cave is now called Ogof Owain Glyndŵr and in the climbing books and the first ascent of that chimney is attributed to him.

Owain Glyndŵr never was caught. He was never betrayed. He never accepted a pardon, even though one was offered when Prince Hal became Henry V. No one knows exactly when he died or where he was buried. He just 'disappeared', perfect for such a hero as it means he can, in accordance with the prophecies of the poets, reappear when the time is right. For Glyndŵr is more than simply an historical personage. He is a legend. He was credited with powers over the weather and the ability to be in two places at once. Like a trickster he miraculously escaped from his enemies

numerous times. He had something of the Robin Hood about him, fighting for the rights of the oppressed Welsh, loyal to the true king (Richard II) against the dastardly usurper (Henry IV). He was a courageous military leader who virtually invented guerilla

The abbot provisioning Owain Glyndŵr. (From *Walk Snowdonia* by Ralph Maddern – with permission.)

warfare and who, for several years, overcame the superior might of his English foes. He was a visionary who imagined a united and independent Wales with just laws, higher education and a flourishing culture. And perhaps, more than anything, Owain Glyndwr fulfilled the role that was prepared for him: as a national redeemer, a 'son of prophecy'. As Shakespeare has him say (in *Henry IV Part I*):

> … Give me leave
> To tell you once again that at my birth
> The front of heaven was full of fiery shapes,
> The goats ran from the mountains, and the herds
> Were strangely clamorous to the frighted fields.
> These signs have marked me as extraordinary,
> And all the courses of my life do show
> I am not in the roll of common man.

Perhaps then, it is not so surprising to find that when, in 1999, the *Sunday Times* asked 100 world leaders, scientists and artists to name the most significant figures of the last 1,000 years, Owain Glyndwr came up as number seven. His war of independence may have failed at the time but his name lives on as a powerful symbol among those who seek justice and liberty.

The Red Bandit s of Mawddwy

In the aftermath of Owain Glyndwr's war of independence and the Wars of the Roses much of Wales was left in a disturbed and lawless state. As a result some of the native peoples of Merionnydd, oppressed and ousted from their settlements, took refuge in the forests and mountains near Cader Idris and lived by plunder, driving off other people's sheep and cattle in the broad light of day. The most infamous of these were a band of outlaws whose hideout was in the remote backcountry of Mawddwy, where huge hills lean over narrow valleys, making travel a challenge at the best of times.

Many of these brigands had red hair, causing some to believe they were descended from the fairy folk. Indeed in the Llanfrothen Legend the fairy mother had predicted that her offspring would spawn a race of men with red hair and prominent noses. As a result they became known as Gwylliaid Cochion Mawddwy, or the Red Bandits of Mawddwy. Some might have called them freedom fighters, striking out at the establishment from their haven in the wild. But for the powers-that-be they were a scourge, villains and vagabonds who had to be destroyed.

At last two pillars of the establishment, John Wynn ap Meredydd of Gwydir Castle and the Sheriff of Merionnydd, Baron Lewis ap Owen (or Baron Owen as he was known), took it upon themselves to deal with this outlaw menace. On Christmas Eve 1554, when snow lay on the ground and when, they rightly assumed, the brigands would be resting in preparation for a Christmas feast, they gathered a posse of well-armed horsemen and headed off into the dark Mawddwy woods, the only sound the clink of soldiers' armour and the muffled drumming of hooves in the snow. In the heart of the forest they found the bandits' deserted camp with the fire still warm and the snow disturbed. Their quarry had fled but had left behind them a trail in the freshly fallen snow. The baron's men followed the tangled chains of footprints through the trees until they caught up with the bandits trapped at the foot of a sheer cliff.

Eighty men were captured, bound and dragged back to the baron who ordered them all to be hung without delay. No due process of law for them. Among those caught were two lads, barely in their teens. Their mother was there too, Lowri, daughter of Gruffydd Llwyd. She pleaded tearfully with the baron for the life of at least her youngest son to be spared. But the sheriff had no pity. He had a reputation for ruthlessness to uphold and on this occasion he would make no exception. Soon the two boys were swinging from trees along with the rest. The distraught Lowri chased after the baron, ripped open her blouse and shouted: 'These yellow breasts have given suck to those who will revenge my sons' blood, and will wash their hands in your heart's blood!'

And sure enough her curse came to pass. Less than a year later, on 12 October 1555, Baron Owen was riding with a bodyguard through the thick woods of Mawddwy on his way home from the Montgomeryshire Assizes. Suddenly a tree fell across the path ahead of them. Before the baron could do anything he and his party were assailed by a shower of arrows. He was struck in the face and then attacked with spears and blades, suffering more than thirty wounds. His son-in-law defended him to the last, though many of his attendants fled on the first onset. It is said that the baron's killers had already gone some distance away before they remembered their mother's threat. So they returned, thrust their swords into the baron's breast, and washed their hands in his heart's blood.

It took three years before those responsible for the baron's murder were rounded up and brought to justice. At a court in Bala in 1558 the last of the Red Bandits of Mawddwy were put on trial and condemned to death. Present too in the courtroom was a certain Lowri, daughter of Gruffydd Llwyd. She managed to avoid the gallows, however, by declaring that she was pregnant, a fact confirmed by a jury of married women.

There are many places which carry a memory of these events in their names to this day. Collfryn, 'the hill of the loss', is the place where the eighty men were hanged on Christmas Eve. Rhos Goch, 'the red or bloody moor', is the mound where their bodies were buried. Llidiart y Barwn, the Baron's Gate, is the place where Lewis Owen was murdered. There is Pont y Lladron, 'the bridge of thieves', Sarn y Gwylliaid, 'the well of the bandits' and Ffynnon y Gwylliaid, 'the well of the robbers'. Not forgetting, of course, Brigands' Inn!

Mar ged the Might y

Stories of mythical giants and giantesses have often been used to explain outstanding natural phenomena – great hills, rocky out-crops, even the mighty mountain of Snowdon itself. Less often are there stories about real people whose lives inspired others to consider them a 'giant of a man' or, in this case, 'a giant of a woman'. Here is one such story.

Marged Ferch Ifan (Margaret, daughter of Evan) was born in 1696, in the Nantlle Valley, and grew into a strapping young woman. She was over 6ft tall, had hair as black as night and hands like shovels. Not only was she exceptionally strong – equal in strength, it was said, to the two strongest men of her time – she was also unusually clever and capable.

When it came to courting she was not interested in the beefy chaps who presented themselves. Rather she went for a meek and mild fellow whom she could easily dominate. A couple of beatings were all he needed to learn who was boss. The first was before the wedding and that set the tone of what was to follow. The second was for drinking and had the effect of turning him into a devout Methodist.

Drws y Coed, a dell at the top of the Nantlle Valley, was, at the time, the home of a thriving copper mine. Mining is thirsty work. So Marged set up a pub at Telyrniau which was exceedingly popular with the miners. Not only did she brew her own ale, she was also effectively her own bouncer. Should any of her customers get out of hand she would silence disorder with a hefty clout round the ear. But Marged had her tender side too. She could play the harp. That is impressive enough but with Marged her talents went further. She had also made the harp and composed many of the tunes she plucked on it too.

Thomas Pennant, author of *A Journey to Snowdon* and *Tours of Wales* in the late eighteenth century, heard tell of Marged's exploits. According to him she was a renowned blacksmith, cobbler and carpenter. She also ran a pack of twelve hunting dogs and was, Pennant said, 'the best hunter of her time'. She was very fond of her dogs. One day one of them strayed into the home of a miner and devoured a huge joint of meat it found on the table. Unsurprisingly the miner was annoyed but what he did was unwise. He killed the dog and threw its body into the river. When Marged found out she was furious. But not only did the miner refuse to compensate her for the loss of the dog (after she'd offered him four times the value of the meat), he also threatened her. Big mistake. One massive left-hook from Marged and he was out cold. She rifled his pockets and found enough money to buy herself another dog!

When the copper mines at Drws y Coed closed down Marged moved two valleys over and worked for the mines that were still operating at Nant Peris. She settled with her husband at the seaward end of Llyn Padarn in the tiny village of Pen Llyn. She made herself a boat and took on the job of transporting the copper ore down the length of Llyn Peris and Llyn Padarn. There were no railways then and the roads were difficult. The lakes offered the best means of transport. Nonetheless it was strenuous labour and ensured that Marged kept up her strength as the years passed. Indeed as a mark of respect she was known as 'the Queen of the Lakes'!

A story is told of how one fellow begged a ride on her boat. But once aboard he refused to pay the tuppance due as the ferry fee. Without further ado Marged tossed him into the water and would not haul him back aboard until he splutteringly agreed that his life was worth a whole guinea.

Mighty Marged was, according to Thomas Pennant, still wrestling young men into her seventies. The scale of her strength – exaggerated perhaps for the sake of the tale – is indicated by the story which tells how she helped to build the bridge of Pont Meibion in Nant Peris. It's made out of a huge single piece of slate. According to the story a gang of young men held up one end of the slate whilst Marged singlehandedly lifted the other. Ah, they don't make them like that any more, man or woman.

Marged it thought to have lived to a ripe old age, well into her nineties, possibly over a hundred. According to legend she was buried under the altar stone in Nant Peris church. But, of course, she didn't die, as her story lives on. A verse from one of the songs written about her says:

> Gentle Marged daughter of Ifan
> Has a big clutch and a little clutch,
> One to drag the dogs from the corner
> Another to break people's bones.

The Mari Jones Walk

Between Cader Idris and the western sea lies the small village of Llanfihangel-y-Pennant. There, in December 1784, a girl was born to the local weaver and his wife. She was christened Mary, Mary Jones, known in Welsh as Mari. Little was there then to suggest she would become perhaps the most famous 'Mary Jones' in history! Her family were devout Calvinistic Methodists and at the age of 8 Mari professed herself a Christian. Until then most Bibles had been in Latin or English, neither of which the poor folk of Llanfihangel-y-Pennant could read. However, now there were Bibles in Welsh, but they were hard to get hold of and expensive to buy.

Mari Jones was a pious girl and when the opportunity came to learn to read at a nearby circulating school – organised by a certain Thomas Charles – she leapt at the chance. She was a diligent student and soon she was frequently walking 2 miles to a neighbour's farm to read out loud their Welsh family Bible. They much appreciated this as none of them could read. However, it only whetted Mari's appetite to have a Bible of her own. But Welsh Bibles were scarce and the nearest place to buy one was in Bala, 25 miles away. Not only that, they cost 3s 6d, which was a fortune to poor families such as Mari's.

However, Mari was determined, and from the age of 9 she did whatever she could to earn a penny – sweeping floors, weeding gardens, running messages, washing steps, looking after children. Eventually, in her sixteenth year, after six years of assiduous saving, she reached her goal. But how was she to get to Bala. There was not a well-used road in that direction, and a lift with the carter would cost her more. So she decided to walk. One summer's morning in 1800 she set out at dawn on her epic walk. Barefoot! She was too poor to afford shoes.

With her purse of money, some bread and cheese wrapped up in a bundle, she walked over the hill, into the Tal-y-Llyn Valley and along the lake. She struck up the steep valley, over the pass and into Cwm Hafod Oer. This was the route taken in 1657 by the first Quaker, George Fox, who had a vision there that God would 'raise up a people to sit under his teaching'. She passed Brithdir and then walked north-east, over the pass at Drws-y-Nant-Uchaf and down to Llyn Tegid. At the far end of the lake she came to the market town of Bala. Whether she did the journey in one day or two is not known, but there is no doubt that she was weary and her feet were sore by the time she reached her destination.

Eventually she found the home of the Reverend Thomas Charles, custodian of the Welsh Bibles. Except that he hadn't any. They were all sold out or promised to others. She was desperate. She blurted out her story – about how she'd saved for six years, how she'd walked 25 miles … and Mr Charles took pity on her. First he made sure she had something to eat and drink. Then, as he was so touched by her tale, he gave her a copy already promised to another. However, some say she had to wait two days for delivery of a new batch of Welsh Bibles and in a gesture of generosity he gave her three for the price of one. There is another version of the story that he gave her his own precious copy of the Bible.

Two copies of Mary Jones' Bible still exist. One is lodged in the archives of the British and Foreign Bible Society in Cambridge. The other is held at the National Library of Wales in Aberystwyth. The copy in Cambridge contains a note, written by Mari in English, on the final page: 'I Bought this in the 16th year of my age. I am Daughter of Jacob Jones and Mary Jones His wife. the Lord may give me grace. Amen.'

Mari made her way back home over the next few days, this time stopping often to read pages from her Bible. On 27 February 1813 she married Thomas Lewis Jones, also a weaver, in the parish church of Tal-y-Llyn and moved to the village of Bryn-crug near Tywyn. She is presumed to have lived a contented life and died on 28 December 1866, aged 82.

As for the Reverend Thomas Charles, he was so inspired by Mari's faith and determination that he urged the Religious Tract Society to establish a new organisation, the British and Foreign Bible Society. This was formed in 1804 with the purpose of dis- tributing Bibles around the world. It is now known as The Bible Society and the tale of Mari Jones is still its founding story.

THE Wreck of the *ROYAL CHARTER*
Based on The Golden Wreck *by Alexander McKee*

The *Royal Charter* was built at the Sandycroft Ironworks on the River Dee and was launched in 1855. She was a large ship, 336ft long and 2,719 tons in weight, and was specially designed to make the long voyage to Australia at the time of the 1851 Gold Rush. The *Royal Charter* was one of the first iron ships and though pri- marily a sailing clipper she also had a steam engine with space for 700 tons of coal. Whenever the winds were calm or contrary the 200hp engine could be started up and the ship would still progress. As a result the *Royal Charter* was one of the fastest ships on the Australia run. She was also one of the most luxurious. Her owners proudly advertised her as 'The magnificent steam clipper *Royal Charter* – Australia in under sixty days.'

In August 1859 she was in Melbourne, Australia, taking on board a cargo of wool, hides, copper and gold. Many of her passengers had made fortunes on the gold fields of Ballarat and were returning with newfound riches to Britain. Gold worth £322,440 was stored in the ship's strongroom, but many people carried their own personal fortunes with them in purses, pockets and money belts. The total gold on that ship would be worth millions of pounds today. She was a veritable treasure ship. The human cargo on that voyage comprised 390 passengers and 112 crew, about 500 souls in all.

The journey back to Britain took them round Cape Horn and was speedy and uneventful. There was dancing, music and amateur dramatics among the saloon passengers and most people were in high spirits. The boat didn't call at any port on route until Queenstown, on the southern Irish coast. There they stopped for a few hours and some of the travellers disembarked. The ship was making record time and the first-class passengers were so pleased they signed a testimonial in praise of the captain, Captain Taylor. He promised them they would be in Liverpool within twenty-four hours.

About 1.30 p.m. on Tuesday, 25 October they came in sight of Holyhead on Anglesey. By then the winds were picking up, and over the mountains of Snowdonia an eerie black haze was lifting rapidly into the air and spreading over the sky. The waves kept rising and soon the winds were blowing a heavy gale. What no one on board knew was that they were sailing into the hurricane of the century, 'a complete horizontal cyclone'. The hurricane was about 300 miles in diameter, moving in a north-easterly direction across Britain. At its centre was a small area of still air, but revolving anti-clockwise around it were maddened winds of up to 100mph. This was Force 12 on the Beaufort Scale and no one had experienced anything like it in British waters before.

Captain Taylor may have briefly considered putting into Holyhead harbour but he'd promised his passengers they'd be in Liverpool that night and he had confidence in his ship. As the boat rounded Anglesey towards Liverpool Bay she drove directly into an easterly wind. With most sails trimmed she was now relying almost entirely on the engine. But as the hurricane advanced the winds began to turn and come from the north, blowing the ship in the direction of the land. By eight o'clock, as huge 50ft waves surged out of the darkness, the *Royal Charter* was pitching and rolling heavily, her bows smacking down onto the waves and sending spray all over the decks. And still the wind was increasing. The first sign of real trouble came when Captain Taylor ordered the helmsman to turn the wheel hard to port to turn the ship away from the shore. Nothing happened. The ship was no longer answering her rudder.

The engine was put on full speed to drive the ship out to sea, but when soundings were taken it became clear that the ship was drifting closer to the unknown shore. The sailors tried to 'stay' the ship by turning her round with the sails. It was extremely hard work climbing the rigging up the wildly reeling masts, being battered by almost solid sheets of water, fumbling with numbed fingers to undo the ropes holding the heavy sails. Unfortunately it was to no avail. The ship continued drifting shorewards. By now Captain Taylor was having frequent consultations with the two other ship captains who were travelling on board as passengers. Just before 11 p.m., as the hurricane rose to its full fury, he gave orders to let go the anchors. When the anchors fell the *Royal Charter* was momentarily checked, but as the enormous waves pounded the ship the chains groaned and stretched with the strain. Meanwhile emergency rockets were sent up and distress guns fired. But it was of no use. Even if the signals had been seen no lifeboat could have reached them now. At about 1.30 a.m. the port cable snapped. An hour later the starboard cable went too. One off-duty captain was heard to say, 'We'll be singing the song of the White Squall tonight!' When asked to explain he made vigorous swimming movements with his arms.

By now there was only one course of action left. The great masts, the rigging and the funnel were all acting as sails before the ferocious winds, helping to move the ship toward land. At about 3 a.m. the captain ordered the metre-thick masts to be cut down. Half an hour after this work began the ship grounded on the shore. By now the saloon was crowded with passengers clinging to each other and crying out in confusion and fear. The captain sent a message down trying to calm the frenzy. He said they'd struck a sandy beach and that as soon as it was light they'd be able to go ashore. There were gasps of relief all round. Unfortunately Captain Taylor got one crucial thing wrong. He thought the tide was turning to go out and would leave the ship high and dry on the shore. But instead it was turning to come in, a fact that would spell the doom of the *Royal Charter*.

At about 6 a.m. the dreadful darkness was slowly diffused by a thin grey light. Eventually they realised they were barely 25 yards from land. But between them and the shore the furious waters seethed and frothed as fallen masts and yardarms leapt about on the breakers. And standing on the rocks just beyond the waves was a man staring out at the great battered ship as if he could not believe his eyes. His roof had been damaged by the fierce winds and he had got up in the dark to fix it. As dawn broke he saw this strange looming shape stranded in the surf and woke up a neighbour to fetch help from the nearby village of Moelfre.

Meanwhile on the boat there was a plan to get a line ashore. A Maltese able seaman, Joseph Rodgers, tied a rope around his waist and prepared to make his swim. Unlike most other sailors he was at home in the water and knew the sea. He examined the scene carefully before choosing his place and moment, then dropped into the raging torrent below. He was three times washed onto the sharp, slippery rocks and three times dragged back into the sea. At last four or five men on the shore, their hands linked together, managed to reach him and pull him to safety. The rope was fastened around a rock. On the ship a bosun's chair was rigged up. The first passengers were about to cross the terrifying watery chasm when a huge wave and the incoming tide combined to raise the ship and smash her down on the jagged rocks close to the shore. The officer in charge of the bosun's chair was trying to get his sweetheart to cross, but she was too frightened. Precious minutes ticked by. Eventually a handful of the crew used the chair

to get themselves ashore. Meanwhile the Reverend Hodge was conducting an impromptu service to prepare the desperate passengers to meet their death. For a moment he managed to calm them. Then, half an hour after being dashed on the rocks, the ship broke in two and a furious, foaming wave roared into the saloon. Many people were swept into the water.

There were a few who survived the boiling cauldron of seething foam and razor-sharp rock, but not many. One man had slept through the storm, the grounding on sand, even the striking of the rocks. He was well rested. Finally he was shaken awake. He dressed, prayed, went up on deck. He spent a long time watching the horrific scene and saw many people weighed down with heavy wet clothes. So he stripped off and, though he could not swim, went overboard and seized hold of a wooden box. He was washed up several times on the rocks and eventually managed to grasp a rope thrown to him by the villagers. Most others died not by drowning but by being brutally dashed upon the rocks. Many had made the mistake of strapping on their money belts full of gold, or filling their pockets with coins. The extra weight made the struggle for survival even harder. One young sailor, Isaac Lewis, must have recognised the shore for he was from the village of Moelfre. Indeed his father was one of the twenty-eight rescuers on the land.

They called to each other but tragically Isaac was swept off the bosun's chair by a giant wave and did not make it home alive.

When the reckoning was done just forty people were plucked out of the waves by the Moelfre villagers. A total of 454 lives were lost that dreadful morning. Not one woman or child survived, nor any officers. All those rescued were wearing minimal clothing, which must have been a factor in their survival. When the villagers realised no one else would be saved they turned their attention to the gleaming gold lodged in the cracks between the rocks. There was a fantastic harvest that grey morning, a harvest of gold and death. Poor men saw more wealth cast up by the sea than they could earn from the sea in years. Within a day or two of the wreck marines were sent to guard the site but still a number of people must have made their fortunes. One woman was counting the coins she'd collected when there was a knock on the door from one of the guards. Quickly she poured the coins into a pot of cockles cooking on the stove. She welcomed him in and offered him cockles and tea.

At the inquest questions were asked about whether the captain had been drunk, but all the surviving crew verified that he was not. In the search to find someone to blame the finger was then pointed at the ship, saying there had been weaknesses in its design. But that accusation could not be proved either. In the end it had to be acknowledged that it was simply the result of an 'Act of God'. However, there was one other potential cause that was never investigated. On its maiden voyage some of the passengers had wantonly killed several albatrosses. Sailors have always regarded albatrosses, with their 10ft wingspan, as special birds. It is thought to be bad luck to kill them, so they never do. Perhaps that was the reason for the terrible tragedy of the *Royal Charter*. We will never know.

7

EPILOGUE

The Pass of the Two Stones

It must be one of the oldest ways in Britain. For millennia it was the only 'easy' east–west route through the Eryri Mountains. Sheer cliffs were an effective barrier on the northern coast. So instead travellers crossed the pass from Rowen in the Conwy Valley to Abergwyngregyn on the Menai Strait. Now known as the 'Roman Road', it was a well-beaten track long before the Romans found it. It should be called the 'Stone Age Way'. It is a 'songline' of ancient Britain, marked by Neolithic burial chambers and a stone circle in the east and the sacred Aber Falls in the west. Powerful Celtic hill forts stand at both ends. To the west of the summit a path forks off to Penmaenmawr, the stone quarry where prized Neolithic axe heads were hewn from the rock to be dispersed all over the land. To the east of the summit are two mighty standing stones: a square grandmother stone (made of pure white quartz) and a tall, dark, pointed grandfather stone. These stones mark a threshold, a gateway between worlds. They give the pass its name: Bwlch y Ddeufaen, the Pass of the Two Stones.

Now electricity pylons stride over this route, but apart from that, little has changed since the Stone Age. The dramatic crag of Tal y Fan still beetles over the stone circle in the north; the high ground of the Carneddau stretches off in the distance to the south. To the east is the coastal plain along which marched the Romans and Normans, enemies of the Cymru. To the south the Conwy ('Holy') river snakes down from the mountains, the Welsh heartland. And to the west over the brow of the pass is the first glimpse of Ynys Môn, Mam Cymru. This was the Otherworld. With the highest concentration of burial chambers anywhere in Britain it was always a sacred island. It became a centre of spiritual power for the Celts, the HQ of the Druids. It was a place to cultivate and concentrate the holy essences that rise from the land. It was a dark and mysterious world that contained within it a brilliant light.

Because so little has changed it's possible to imagine the procession of people who trod this ancient path. The vast majority of them are, of course, nameless.

⌘

Perhaps the first was the hunter who, 12,000 years ago, stayed the night before in Kendrick's Cave at the edge of the Great Orme, carving the moon on a shining horse's jawbone. He'd been watching the snow melt on the high ground to the west. Now there was a dark strip where the ice had gone showing a way through the mountains. He wanted to see what was beyond the age-old wall of ice. In the morning he would walk upriver to the crossing place. Then he would climb. He knew he would find a pass. He knew he would make a path.

Six thousand years later there was a track over the pass to the big stone head, Penmaenmawr. This was the way of the axe-head carrier. Pen was the best place to find stone for shaping into axes, knives and arrowheads. The stone peddlar picked out the best and carried a heavy bundle of roughs through the pass and down to the holy river. Usually he headed toward the rising sun along the coastal plain. Easier that way. Until he came to the next big waterway, Deva, river of the goddess. There he would hand on his load, exchange it for skins or carved bone. Occasionally he walked south upriver into the mountains. Harder work this. But he would always find someone who wanted his precious stones. He heard some were traded to the far ends of the Great Island herself.

⌘

A thousand years later and the stone workers were shaping bigger stones, raising them into standing sentinels, guardians, waymarkers; lifting and crafting them into mighty tombs for the dead. The greatest of them all were the two gatekeepers marking the way and giving the pass its name: Bwlch y Ddeufaen.

Five hundred years after and just below the Two Stones a circle of standing stones was raised. Here people gathered – at sunrise and sunset, solstices and equinoxes. The leader of the ceremony, the shaman-bard, chanted a long song: summoning the spirits, speaking to the ancestors, thanking the earth mother, addressing the star gods. The people joined in. Sometimes they swayed and stamped. Sometimes they shouted and cheered. Balance was restored. Survival was ensured.

Another few hundred years passed. Further down the hill a settlement grew. A series of terraces sprouted roundhouses, enclosures and, cleverly hidden, a bijou chamber for the dead. This was a place to feel peace and stillness whilst communing with the spirits of the departed. And maybe to reflect on how to live. Many stopped on their way over the mountain. So many that later, 100 years or so, another burial chamber was built, more prominent, available to passers-by. This was the public burial chamber, the one to which people came from far and wide. It was linked to 'awen' (inspiration) and became known as Maen y Bardd, Stone of the Bards. The people in this settlement were outliers of the Mona Druids watching over the border and guarding access to the sacred isle.

From the time of the first stone peddlar 100 generations had passed. But no one's name was passed down. All who'd lived and died were forgotten, remembered only as the all-encompassing 'ancestors'. But from two thousand and some hundred years ago onwards, a few names survived. Bendigeidfran, Bran the Blessed, the giant king of the Island of the Mighty; Math, son of Mathonwy and Gwydion, son of Dôn. These mythic characters, descendants of the gods, if they existed, must have come this way. As did those nameless ones who came from all over Gaul and Britannia to study with Druids.

And then came the Romans. How did Suetonius Paulinus and his troop feel when they crested the brow and first caught sight of Mona, the Druid Isle? Trepidation, perhaps? Determination? And how about those who watched them from high on the crags? Did they send fleet-footed messengers ahead to warn the Druids? The sight of the Roman Army must have filled them with dread. It was to bring to an end a way of life that had endured, changing slowly, for 3,000 years. Now things would change quickly. Now we would remember names. Now history would begin.

The Pass of the Two Stones was the most direct route between the Roman forts at Caer (Chester) and Segontium (Caernarfon). So maybe Emperor Macsen came this way to claim Elen, the bride of his dreams. The threshold guardians who lived here must have been among the first to hear of the boy Merlin's prophecy. Later Merlin would have come this way. And Taliesin. Why, after all, was it called Maen y Bardd? Perhaps Taliesin, bard of bards, used to stop here, sit in the burial chamber, say a prayer for the dead, make an offering, invite inspiration for a new poem.

Maelgwn Gwynedd had a court at Aberffraw on Ynys Môn and one at Deganwy on the mouth of the Conwy river. So he must have travelled this way too. And in the wake of Maelgwn, the saints, those he clashed with, the ones he endowed with money and land – Cybi, Deiniol, Padarn, Beuno … Perhaps his old enemy Gildas walked this way, and later the scholars Giraldus Cambrensis and Geoffrey of Monmouth. Arthur, of course, must have ridden through here. He went everywhere, after all. As well as the noble Gruffydd the Wanderer and the mighty Llywelyn the Great. Wicked King John on his way to burn down the cathedral in Bangor came this way, as did, from the Welsh point of view, the even more wicked Edward I. And Owain Glyndwr, 'son of prophecy', who came so close to uniting Wales, must have paused here below the crags, looked at the gleaming river snaking down from the heartlands, looked east along the coastline towards his Norman enemies, looked west to the Mother Island ... and seen such beauty, felt such love.

What a pageant has paraded through this Pass of the Two Stones. Probably none stopped for long. All were walking or riding, keen to make it quickly over the mountain moorland to the safety of the valley below. But many must have paused a moment, perhaps to shelter and pray in Maen y Bardd, perhaps to lean against one of the two great stones. The light from so many faces has been reflected on those obelisks. Most are unremembered. A few names ring out still. It is, alas, 'an insubstantial pageant faded'. But if you have read this book then now at least you know some of their stories.

BIBLIOGRAPHY

Barber, Chris & Pykitt, David, *Journey to Avalon* (Blorenge Books)

Blake, Steve & Lloyd, Scott, *The Keys to Avalon: The True Location of Arthur's Kingdom Revealed* (Element)

Borrow, George, *Wild Wales: The People, Language and Scenery* (Century)

Breverton, Terry, *Owain Glyndŵr: The Story of the Last Prince of Wales* (Amberley)

Bromwich, Rachel, *Trioedd Ynys Prydein/The Welsh Triads* (University of Wales Press)

Charles-Edwards, T.M., *Wales and the Britons 350–1064* (Oxford University Press)

Clarke, Gillian (trans.), *One Moonlit Night* (Pont Books)

Clarke, Lindsay, *Parzival and the Stone from Heaven* (Voyager)

Dames, Michael, *Merlin and Wales: A Magician's Landscape* (Thames and Hudson)

Davies, R.R., *The Revolt of Owain Glyndŵr* (Oxford University Press)

Davies, Sioned (trans.), *The Mabinogion* (Oxford University Press)

Emerson, P.H., *Welsh Fairy Tales and Other Stories* (Kessinger Publishing Reprint)

Geoffrey of Monmouth, *The History of the Kings of Britain* (Penguin)

Gildas the Wise, *On the Ruin of Britain* (Serenity)

Gerald of Wales, *The Journey Through Wales/Description of Wales* (Penguin)

Godwin, Malcolm, *The Holy Grail: It's Origins, Secrets and Meaning Revealed* (Labyrinth)

Gruffydd, Elfed, *Llŷn* (Gwasg Carreg Gwalch)

Gwyndaf, Robin, *Welsh Folk Tales* (National Museum of Wales)

Harris, Mike, *Awen, The Quest of Celtic Mysteries* (Skylight Press)

Henken, Elissa R., *National Redeemer: Owain Glyndŵr in Welsh Tradition* (University of Wales Press)

Jenkins, D.E., *Bedd Gelert: Its Facts, Fairies and Folklore* (Friends of St Mary's Church, Beddgelert)

Jenkyn Thomas, W., *The Welsh Fairy Book* (University of Wales Press)

Jenkyn Thomas, W., *More Welsh Fairy and Folk Tales* (University of Wales Press)

Jones, Gwyn & Jones, Thomas (trans.), *The Mabinogion* (Everyman Library)

Jones, Gwyn, *Welsh Legends and Folk-Tales* (Puffin Books)

Lynch, Frances, *Gwynedd: A Guide to Ancient and Historic Wales* (HMSO)

Maddern, Ralph, *Walk in Magnificent Snowdonia* (Focus Publications)

Maddern, Ralph, *Walk Snowdonia: Ancient Trackways, Roman Roads, Packhorse Trails* (Focus Publications)

Main, Laurence, *The Spirit Paths of Wales* (Cicerone Press)

Matthews, John, *Taliesin: Shamanism and the Bardic Mysteries in Britain and Ireland* (Aquarian Press)

Middleton, Haydn, *Island of the Mighty: Stories of Old Britain* (Oxford Myths and Legends)

Owen, Elias, *Welsh Folklore* (reprinted by Forgotten Books)

Parry-Jones, D., *Welsh Legends and Fairy Lore* (B.T. Batsford)

Pennant, Thomas, *A Tour in Wales: Volume II* (Bridge Books)

Pennar, Meirion (trans.), *The Black Book of Carmarthen* (Llanerch Enterprises)

Perrin, Jim, *Snowdon, The Story of a Welsh Mountain* (Gomer)

Rees, Alwyn & Rees, Brinley, *Celtic Heritage: Ancient Traditions in Ireland and Wales* (Thames and Hudson)

Ross, Anne, *Folklore of Wales* (Tempus)

Ross, Anne & Robins, Don, *The Life and Death of a Druid Prince* (Guild Publishing)

Senior, Michael, *Eryri: The Story of Snowdonia* (Gwasg Carreg Gwalch)

Sheppard-Jones, Elisabeth, *Stories from Welsh History* (John Jones)

Sheppard-Jones, Elisabeth, *Stories of Wales* (John Jones)

Skidmore, Ian, *A Gwynedd Anthology* (Christopher Davies)

Steele, Philip, *Llyn Cerrig Bach: Treasure from the Iron Age* (Oriel Ynys Môn)

Stewart, R.J. *The Prophetic Vision of Merlin* (Arkana)

Styles, Showell, *Welsh Walks and Legends* (John Jones)

Watkins, Graham, *Walking with Welsh Legends: Northern Wales* (Llygad Gwalch)

Williamson, Robin, *The Craneskin Bag: Celtic Stories and Poems* (Canongate)